# THE NEW PROPHETIC GENERATION

APOSTLE SHERMAN D. FARMER

*The New Prophetic Generation*
Copyright © 2013 Sherman D. Farmer

All rights reserved. No part of this book may be reproduced, distributed or transmitted in any form by any means, graphics, electronics, or mechanical, including photocopy, recording, taping, or by any information storage or retrieval system, without permission in writing from the publisher except in the case of reprints in the context of reviews, quotes, or references.

Unless otherwise indicated, scripture quotations are from the Holy Bible, King James Version. All rights reserved.

The Message. Copyright © by Eugene H. Patterson, 1993, 1994, 1995. All rights reserved.

Published by: Purposely Created Publishing Group™

Printed in the United States of America

ISBN: 0-692-29749-9
ISBN-13: 978-0-692-29749-0

---

Special discounts are available on bulk quantity purchases by book clubs, associations and special interest groups. For details email: sales@PurposelyCreatedPG.com or call (866) 674-3340.

*For more information, log onto*
www.PurposelyCreatedPG.com

# DEDICATION

I would like to dedicate this book to my parents, Deborah and Elton Senior; my siblings, Elton Jr. and Sharon; my Apostolic Team: Jerome, Justin, Cheronda, Arnetta, and Tony; my countless sons and daughters; New Gibeah Ministries for Christ; Redeeming Touch of Love Ministries (Alicia and Ward Corbin); my biological mother, Delores Farmer; my grandmother, Beatrice Farmer Johnson; Elder George Chase, I will always be indebted to your tutelage. Thank you for handling me as a prophetic father should; and Prophet Brian Mosley, thank you for taking me under your wing and making me a true son!

And a special thank you to Tieshena Davis and Tarinna Terrell for assisting me with the vision that God has given.

Agape,

*Apostle Farmer*

# CONTENTS

Introduction ........................................................... ix

## Chapter 1: Genesis

My Prophetic Genesis ................................................ 1
My Prophetic Growth ................................................ 12
My Prophetic Gift ..................................................... 22

## Chapter 2: Family

The Premiere Ministry of God ................................... 29

The Assignment of Mankind is Through the Conduit
of Generations ......................................................... 37

   a.  Assignments & Deadlines ................................. 39

   b.  Operation Urgency:
       From Generation to Generation ...................... 42

The Revelations About Men is Through the Conduit
of Genealogies ......................................................... 47

   a.  Apostolic Revelation ........................................ 53

## Chapter 3: From Levi to Jesus

*Prophetic Generations, Genealogies and Gospels*

   a.  1st Generation: Levi ......................................... 55

   b.  2nd Generation: Kohath .................................. 59

   c.  3rd Generation: Amram (Jochebed) ................ 63

    d.   4th Generation: Moses (Miriam and Aaron)....... 66

Further Confirmation of the First Prophetic Family......... 68

Conclusion of the First Prophetic Family............................ 73

The Return of the Kohathite Anointing:
John the Baptist (Zechariah)................................................. 76

The New Kohathite Generation: Jesus Christ................... 78

The Cycle of the New Generational Deliverance............. 81

## Chapter 4: Capitals & Diasporas

*The Relevance & Revelation of Capitals & Diasporas*

    a.   The First Capital of Humanity:
           The Edenic Environment..................................... 85

    b.   The First Diaspora of Humanity:        88
           The Adamic Generation...............................................

    c.   The Genesis of Levitical Diasporas..................... 93

Levi, the Human Tithe of God............................................. 97

Further Study of the Kohathite Diaspora....................... 102

## Chapter 5: Nomad or Civilized?

*The Connection of Old & New Prophetic Capitals*

    a.   Review of the Original Prophetic Capitals.......... 109

    b.   The Band of Prophets Paradigm (Gibeah and
           Ramah).................................................................. 112

    c.   The Sons of Prophets Paradigm (Gilgal, Bethel
           & Jericho)................................................................ 119

    d.    Prophetic Activity in Judah (David).......................... 122

Modern Day Examples of Prophetic Diasporas: Antioch & Ephesus............................................................ 124

The Greatest Modern Day Example of Prophetic Capital: Corinth................................................................. 127

Conclusion.......................................................................... 130

## Chapter 6: Sons or Bastards?

*The Reemergence of true Prophetic Fathers and Sons*

    a.    The Incidents at Gibeah and Ramah..................... 133

    b.    The Incidents at Gilgal, Bethel and Jericho......... 139

The Correlation of Spiritual Adoption & Prophetic Sons..................................................................................... 150

A Prophetic Father's Words Over His Prophetic Son...... 154

## Chapter 7: The Goal is God!

My Prophetic Generation..................................................... 161

Decrees and Declarations.................................................... 165

Conclusion.............................................................................. 171

## About the Author                            179

# INTRODUCTION

All parenting, natural and spiritual alike, is for the purpose of safety and sanity within the assignments of God. Spiritual family is a place of accountability and stability, where fathers can love their sons and sons can love their fathers. When this returns, the hoax will dissipate and more credibility will manifest. True strategy for prophetic intercession is being exhorted here. The cry for the return of proper spiritual homes, filled with legitimate spiritual families that are committed to the emergence of true prophetic people, is the summons that we need to pray for. The spirit of a prophetic bastard season is surely over!

Sons, find your fathers. Fathers, find your sons!

# 1

# Genesis

## MY PROPHETIC GENESIS
### The Revelation – You're a Prophet!
*Isaiah Chapter 6*

Like the first book of the Bible, everything has a genesis. And my prophetic genesis starts with music. The journey of music-genesis begins 1985. I am twelve years old and a graduate from elementary school. On the eve of graduation, I follow a girl to her aunt's church for a choir rehearsal as a means of impressing her. Instead, my apprehension became music and God. It was a match made in heaven because it came from heaven. Instantly, I fell in love with gospel music. But greater in love I found the Lord. And both loves were found on the same night.

One pivotal prophesy given years later, in this very church, was through a woman of God who revealed that I would travel, sing and play the piano similar to her ministry.

## The New Prophetic Generation

This prophecy eventually does come to pass. I subsequently develop greater aspirations of becoming a national contemporary gospel artist, and gospel music came alive within me. The conception of a dream took place. The goal of this dream was singing, playing piano, and writing songs. My plans for implementing the dream were very extensive. I would teach music as a main source of income until my music ministry became known. These first steps of trailblazer breadcrumbs led me to the beginnings of prophetic destiny.

Moving forward, it's now 1988 and time to initiate the dream. The first task at hand was the need to create a singing group. I knew there was something special in my writing. I was bubbling with inspiration and was convinced my music would become stellar hits! So I drafted and persuaded a few neighborhood friends to join my campaign. One of the friends was the very girl that I followed to church. She and another childhood friend were the first members. The name of the group became Mission. And every mission needs a strategic plan, so when we arrived at high school, my first plan of action was to find other members who would join. After gathering the first members of the group, we evolved over time. Eventually Mission would become Testify, and in 2003, Testify emerged as Divine Compliment. In retrospect, I had no idea what I was doing when I first started this group, but God did. And He uses everything—both good and bad—as a means of providing the necessary roadway to Him and destiny.

I was confident in God's declaration that music would be first and pastoring would follow. What I must mention, however, is how this plan evolves. Music was indeed first, but preaching didn't blossom in this journey until ten years later. The evolution to this plan from music to pulpit ministry was immediately realized after my initial calling to preach.

What I discovered between the growth span of music and my preaching genesis becomes altogether different. I was like Abraham, moving from a known land to something much unknown. The blueprints of my new destiny were formed from a renewed mind, but that did not change how my old nature tried to weaken the new thoughts; I would often fight the propensity of reverting to my old sins. Regardless of my sins, I have witnessed how the plan of God over your life never fails.

The plan of God for my life is truly God's masterpiece. Despite my struggles, I had God. And what I have with God is truly a plan from God. The problem with the plan of God was in the order He wanted me to carry out each event. In hindsight, it appeared as if the plan just wasn't in the right order, but in time God helped me with the order.

In late summer of 2003, Divine Compliment was in Detroit, Michigan. We had the opportunity to participate at the Gospel Music Workshop of America (GMWA). Earlier that morning, before the performance, I went onto the balcony of our hotel room. In gratitude to God, I began to weep with thanksgiving. In the midst of giving thanks and shedding tears, I saw a very long process towards the dream unfolding. I could visibly see myself at the precipice, but what eventually happens was more like a nightmare. Hindsight is truly 20/20. Now I know that it was God protecting what He was investing in me. Back then, I felt I was totally out of order, and I felt that I had missed God, to put it plainly.

Later that evening, Divine Compliment ministered as planned at the workshop. After our performance, the individual responsible for organizing the engagement took us into a private room to talk further. He then explained that we did it! We had reached our destination. What was that destination? It was a music career with a well-known record label. The group was in tears. All we could do was praise God while crying relentlessly. As a sign of good intentions, he also gave the group VIP access to that same label's listening party, scheduled later on that night. When we arrived at the listening party, sheer amazement was our unanimous view. All the well-known music ministries and singers of the gospel industry that I grew up listening to are in the very room that we are escorted into. I remember saying, *"This is Canaan."* It was Canaan, but it was the period to spy the land, not to actually take it.

We left GMWA with the feeling of accomplishment. Our excitement was overflowing. We kept saying to ourselves, *"All those long rehearsals and sessions has finally paid off. All the money spent was not in vain."* We kept discussing. *"This dream is about to come true."* Well the dream didn't come true! A few weeks later, everything changed drastically. Before we could get to the table to seal the deal, a sudden merger between the label and a larger distribution subsidiary occurred. As a means of starting fresh, the label decided to drop its new talent.

"Embarrassment" puts it mildly. All the sharing with family and friends made us look like liars. When I sat there on the other end of the phone and received the bad news, hopelessness began to tug at my heart. In fact, the dream felt shattered. I thought to myself, *"What now?"* I had put all I had into this plan and it bottomed out! No, it backfired! Afterwards, the questions came and I didn't have any answers.

If prophets would be honest, they, too, have been here before. A dream sometimes can be misinterpreted or put in the wrong sequence. We can mishandle the information God gives us. We can even add our own interpretation to what God has said. Genesis 16 tells how Abraham and Sarah distorted and polluted their prophecy. So why can't we? And if I had to use my imagination and listen to Sarah and Abraham testify today, like them, I would have to admit that I also mishandled my prophecies. This period of my life was one of the major lessons in the prophetic. It was a time of great learning mixed with great shame. I was highly embarrassed having told everyone I knew that we had finally reached our goal. The goal was more like a mirage in a desert.

However, when God has a plan, His plan will commence whether we can see it properly or not. God has a unique way of ensuring correct navigation to our proper destination. Failures, frustrations and fumbled attempts all play part of his providential care. Being very transparent, I was a novice to the spirit and the voice of God. I felt like I was fumbling around in the dark, making everything seem very stressful. I was working hard to keep an appearance of being calm and in control while around the group, but inwardly, I was holding onto what appeared to be a very dead dream. As far as I was concerned, I led the group in the wrong direction. Knowing that a group isn't any stronger than its leader, I felt that I had let the group down! What I learned about my destiny was that music was just a roadway, but God was the only way. For the accuracy of God's plan truly started on the night of my prophetic genesis.

## The New Prophetic Generation

Let's briefly rewind. It's 1992 and I am abruptly brought out of a deep sleep with a feeling of urgency. I heard very clear instructions: "Read Isaiah Chapter 6." The voice also said, "This chapter has thirteen verses." Now I know why this voice gave me an explanation of the number of verses. This was my very first experience of using the gift of the word of knowledge. So when the voice spoke to me, it didn't take long to grasp what God was saying. It was a great implication. God was calling me to preach.

The message of the chapter presented an obvious summon to a greater level of ministry. It refers to a man who God prophetically commissions, and this commission comes during one of the worst periods of this man's life. A close relative dies within the same year, so not only is Isaiah mourning the loss of his relative, but the relative is the national leader of Israel. The leader is the deceased king, Uzziah. Even in the midst of Isaiah's suffering and mourning, there's still an effortless compliance. So Isaiah becomes the sole prophetic candidate of scripture who exhibits willingness to serve in the prophetic ministry.

What I love most about this call is the transparency Isaiah exudes. Isaiah is quick to comply with the manifest presence of God. Isaiah does not have the running away from God testimony. When God manifested, Isaiah immediately responded. He told the truth about his condition concerning sin. This is why Isaiah is unlike any other prophet of the Old Testament. Their dialogues with God about the prophetic typically comes with resentment and reservations, but Isaiah's account is of such great uniqueness. He was the only prophet who went towards his call instead of running away from it. And after God allowed him to hear a discussion in heaven, Isaiah spoke this very famous response:

**Also I heard the voice of the Lord, saying, whom shall I send, and who will go for us? Then said I, Here am I; send me (Isaiah 6:8).**

I asked God, "Are you calling me to preach? And if so, please confirm it!" God answered very quickly. My prophetic genesis experience was on a late Saturday night leading into an early Sunday morning. I remember going to church later. When the preacher stood to proclaim the message he said, "Turn with me to the book of Isaiah, Chapter 6." He then gave the title of his message, *Accepting the Call of God*. Hearing the text and title, I instantly jumped up to share my experience from the night before. God would then use this local body of believers as my principle eyewitnesses concerning my first public declaration. I proclaimed from that day forward: God is calling me to preach!

However, saying yes is the easy part. Enduring storms because of your call to ministry is the hard part. In many ways, I would have an experience parallel to Isaiah's. I, too, would lose a very close relative. It was the very first time I heard the Lord respond. This was very different from God awakening me out of my sleep with adamant instructions. This time he would answer me directly. Numbers 23:19 says, "He is not a man that He should lie!" For the word of the Lord surely came to pass.

In 1995, unfortunate and sudden news concerning the status of a particular loved one had come to my family's attention. My mother had been incarcerated majority of my life. We received a random knock at the door. It was one of my mother's friends.

In fact it was a street buddy. He unknowingly was the harbinger of her condition and bad news. The news was that she was in a coma. He came over to pay his respects and prayers as if we had prior knowledge, but the city jail didn't even bother to contact us. We had to learn it firsthand from what I adamantly consider a stranger. My grandmother and I looked at the individual as we stood in disbelief. After calling the local hospital, only to discover that she was indeed sick, we now had to prepare ourselves for the worst. Before I went to see her, I asked God if she would live. God responded very clearly: "Prepare your heart because she will not return." This was my first prophetic experience of hearing God's voice. *What a way to begin my direct prophetic lessons.*

The prophetic reminder of Isaiah's own storyline was staring me dead in the face! On November 13, 1995, my mother passed away from complications due to AIDS and ovarian cancer. It felt like my family just couldn't get a break. My great-grandmother was a faithful prophetess and evangelist, but she died from massive degree burns due to a house fire. My grandmother, my great-grandmother's daughter, lost her husband from a brutal murder when he was shot during a robbery right before her and my mother's very eyes. These moments of darkness overshadows our family and leads to many addictions. These situations partially concern my mother's downward spiral into drugs, crime and incarceration. And the loss of my mother dying in jail with AIDS and cancer was like a cherry on top of an unwanted sundae. These events tried to discourage my life.

Instead of being discouraged by her death, I found encouragement in hearing God. Her death was the moment that I heard and seen him, greater than I ever had before. Of course these were sad times, but my joy somehow remained full. And even within the piercing darkness of my sorrows, the Lord caused greater shifts to occur within my spirit. As I reflect on my past, I now see these moments of sadness as tools to create the beginning fragments to a larger puzzle. This puzzle and picture concerns my prophetic destiny. For pain and discomfort is certainly part of any prophet's road. I can candidly answer the question about Nazareth. Can any good thing come out of Nazareth? *Yes, because I did!*

I came out of my Nazareth with Jesus because I kept my sanity by staying close to God. I focused heavily on reading the Bible and learning scriptures. It was my comfort through the loss of my mother. I also created fusions of music with biblical passages during my vast hours of worship. Through my personal praise and worship, I was further led into the prophetic. Ever since my early church days, as a pre-teen, I've always been a praise and worshipper at heart, but I didn't know that the talent of music would connect with being Levitical and prophetic. And I didn't know that this talent would connect me more with the Spirit. This personal process was creating a divine hybrid to my dream. The hybrid was birthing my unique prophetic expression through music and ministry.

And so it was the same with this storm of personalized pain. It became like a boot camp for my prophetic training. Just as a cake is nothing if all ingredients are not compiled properly, so are the fragments likened unto a mere calling and dream. You can have all the right components, but if no one is available to help with the understanding then all you have is an incomplete puzzle. Never will you have the manifestation of the cake if you don't learn how to bake. So as a solution, instinctively, I knew that I needed someone to guide me. I began the search for a leader. And the criterion was very simple; I was looking for someone to understand how to manage me, my gifts and purpose. This task took time, but God came in on time with the right leader.

Ironically, one of my closest friends, also a member of Testify, dated a preacher. His name was Elder George Chase, but we preferred to call him "Overseer." So when I shared my need for seasoned spiritual leadership with her, she arranged a meeting. It was from this strategic connection that I acquired my very first prophetic father. This man of God took the time to care for my spiritual development.

He then became the overseer of Testify and my personal mentor for what I thought would be just for the preaching ministry, but what God had in mind was something more. As a means of development, I would follow him to a Bible school that he was attending in Laurel, Delaware. The travel time from Washington D.C. to Delaware took approximately four hours, round trip.

We traveled this commute twice a week. Each trip was my opportunity to probe him concerning his prophetic ability. I repeatedly asked him why he would prophesize to everyone in the group, except me. I felt that I should have been the first to receive a prophetic word. After all, I was the leader. How little did I understand ministry, as well as the fact that a prophet can only speak when God says speak. I didn't know any better, so I kept ranting and raving each time we traveled.

My inquisition was not a form of rudeness. I don't want you to get that impression. I truly admired and appreciated his prophetic gift, but I was working with a one-track mind. I was only interested in what God had to say about my destiny. *But revelation about destiny has its own appointed time.* Overseer was very careful as to how he handled the release of prophetic words. He knew the answer to my question all along. However, it was not yet time to know. What I must also mention is that Overseer's words always came to pass. He would speak thoroughly, and his prophetic accuracy was powerful. Though I continuously inquired with eagerness, he didn't budge.

But I wasn't going to give up. I kept nagging and asking. I was relentless in my stand. So finally he appeared to capitulate. What I know now is that he released it at the right time, and his response was very calculated. He very gently stated, "Your assignment is very large and you must mature before God will reveal it in its entirety." I didn't feel that response was satisfactory! It only made me thirstier. Knowing my personality, he then looked at me with a big smile. What followed were the words I needed to hear; he said to me: *"You're a prophet!"*

# MY PROPHETIC GROWTH
## The Revelation of the Emerging Prophetic-Teacher and Chief-Levite
### 2 Chronicles 5:11-14

"You're a prophet" was music to my ears! But I processed this statement vaguely and vogue. It was vague because I truly didn't understand the totality of the purpose of a prophet. Vogue because it felt like I had just purchased a new outfit. I felt like my nakedness of not knowing was now over. Like a new garment, I was not yet ready to wear this trendy thought. I finally had an idea of my mantle, but I had to present this follow-up question: What is a prophet? He then responded, saying, "Go home and pray about it." Again, the answers returned to the status of unsatisfactory. I was more frustrated than ever. The glimpses provided only whet my appetite, and like an appetizer before the meal, what I really wanted was the main course!

When I arrived home, instead of prayer, I sat down on the edge of my bed. There, I got a brilliant idea which was actually a leading from the Spirit. My thought process prompted me towards the mini concordance in the back of my Bible. The inclination came. *Lookup any and every word associated with "prophet."* And that's exactly what I did. Every scripture concerning prophets, prophesying, prophecy, and those related to the prophetic became an intensive study project. What started on that day became the premise for this book.

Almost twenty years of revelation and factual information begins with this testimony! And now, in this season of my life, God has instructed the time of release. I am now sharing this knowledge with you.

Studying God's word about the prophetic is what protected me from prophetic prostitution, which is exactly how it sounds. It is when people are manipulated to sell out in their prophetic gift (like a literal prostitute would to a client). Those in prophetic prostitution become manipulators of prophetic ministry because they have not been trained in their gifting properly. And I was determined not to be pimped by other undeveloped prophets. I demanded by my personal convictions that my gift would remain pure and be used for its original intention, so I sought God for more clarity.

Instead of reading other books about people's revelations or thoughts, God instructed me on the backside of the desert. When I got ahold of the information, it began to explode within me. The topical studying cultured the prophetic leader and teacher inside of me. I was quickened by the words of scripture, and my tension spans of intense study rapidly grew. I could tolerate late nights, neglecting sleep and disregard for food and rest. The excitement of digesting the prophetic and learning the word became enough meat. As I read various passages of scripture, the Lord would speak heavily to me, and a faithful student I became.

I took in-depth notes as the Holy Spirit instructed. This was my very own private Prophecy 101 class. It was a wilderness training experience. Thousands of notebooks, notepads, highlighters, and pens were slaughtered and sacrificed—all because of God's speaking and revelation receiving. My style of writing, thinking and processing the word of God was fluid and full of flare. The experience was exciting, yet challenging, while at the same time very unique. Even my mentor confirmed this process. As I shared what I had learned, he would sit back and marvel. Often he would say how very different I was! He also told me that I was a master-teacher. Again, in hindsight I've realized that the more responsible I became, the more God would allow the puzzle to unfold. I can truly testify. Once you accept the call and study your calling, God will increase your understanding!

I have to again thank God for Overseer, my first prophetic father. His patience, tolerance and teachings are still part of my very being. He would often sit for hours and allow me to express myself. Sometimes I would even call him in the middle of the night. That is the makings of a great spiritual father. He took time for me, while simultaneously heavily developing himself. And he carefully watched over me as I took my very first prophetic steps. I felt just like a toddler. A child constantly removed from his stroller and placed on the floor as an eager parent awaits the first steps. Honestly speaking, it didn't take long for me to walk because I had a knowledgeable father. On one particular night, a specific scripture given changed my life. This scripture provides the next pointer on my prophetic compass. Overseer asked if I'd read 2 Chronicles 5: 11-14. "No, I don't think so," I responded. And when I read the pericope, another doorway to prophetic destiny opened:

**And it came to pass, when the priests were come out of the holy place: (for all the priests that were present were sanctified, and did not then wait by course: also the Levites**

**which were the singers, all of them of Asaph, of Heman, of Jeduthun, with their sons and their brethren, being arrayed in white linen, having cymbals and psalteries and harps, stood at the east end of the altar, and with them a hundred and twenty priests sounding with trumpets:) It came to pass, as the trumpeters and singers were as one, to make one sound to be heard in praising and thanking the Lord; and when they lifted up their voice with the trumpets and cymbals and instruments of music, and praised the Lord, saying, for He is good; for His mercy endureth forever: that then the house was filled with a cloud, even the house of the Lord; so that the priests could not stand to minister by reason of the cloud: for the glory of the Lord had filled the house of God. (2 Chronicles 5:11-14, KJV).**

My overseer discerned something special within me. He saw the prophetic. He saw musical ability. And he also saw the teaching ability. These gifts were all merging into the manifold mantle of my calling. After reading these verses, he shared exactly what the Lord said: "God has called you to be a prophet and a Chief Levite within the music ministry." And after the prophetic word was finished, I immediately gave witness. Within my spirit, I bared witness that his utterance was true. For in my private time, God had spoken something similar. The confirmation had come!

I must say this! I am a firm believer that both salvation and the Holy Spirit are spiritual fundamentals. And before any biblical interpretation and prophetic clarity can begin, one's study and prayer life has to be developed. I can testify that this helps with sobriety! And because of the Holy Ghost's presence in my life, I could see that God was navigating my spirit. I could also understand that God was teaching me how to navigate in the Spirit. At the same time, God was using my overseer to protect me from the potentials of prophetic error in the Spirit. For I know now that I was very fortunate to have such a great example—a true father indeed! He was the first male figure in my life.

Prior to music, preaching and the prophetic ministry, I felt my life was worthless. My natural genesis and journey of life started in 1973. I was born in one of the oldest low-income housing projects of Northeast Washington, D.C. I was a child filled with hurts and pains due to an alcoholic grandmother, drug-addicted mother, and an unknown father. If it wasn't for God and the talent of music, I don't think I would have survived. The gift of prophecy played a major role in my survival as well.

When I activated the music talents and prophetic gifting, it transported me to greater realms. I left my present reality behind. Anytime I touched the keyboard and my Bible, the prophetic-teacher and worship leader came forth. Then my reality of pain became obsolete and my problems disappeared. As long as the unction and the oil upon me flowed, I was protected and I was happy. This is why I am an advocate for heavy prayer, worship and study times with God. It's important for any spiritual leader, *especially* one assuming the position of prophet.

In retrospect, God designed this season as a means of preservation. These shifts were backdrops of divine and prophetic development. Greater glimpses of glory emerged when I worshipped God in spite of my present predicament. When I faced my reality, all I could see was pain and the environmental prison. The experience was an oxymoron—two different worlds, if you will. On one hand, I was free in the Spirit during worship. On the other, I felt bound when I looked at my physical surroundings. Working through the pendulum of problems versus being prophetic allowed me to thoroughly understand how these experiences shaped my Levitical, prophetic and master teacher assignments.

No longer did my natural birth scream futile, and my pains no longer had acute affects. Progressively, I received divine satisfaction. I walked into my new identity with Holy Ghost joy. I had a regimen of practicing the prophetic. I kept speaking it over myself daily. "You are a prophet! You're a teacher! You're a Chief Levite in music ministry." And then something else tugged at my heart, so I said it as well. "And one day you'll become a pastor!"

And just think: All of this began from time spent with God, time within his word, and even through prophetic instruction given by Overseer. The scripture Overseer released is what propelled greater increments of destiny, which was uploading more than I ever would have imagined. But with this information comes much responsibility! The list grew longer: a prophet, teacher, Chief Levite in Music Ministry, plus pastor, which all revealed a high call. It also confirmed my overseer's initial words on the day he first explained that I was a prophet. Simply put, there was no time for failure or folly! I had to learn obedience, submission and receptivity fast. As we know, unto whom much is given, much is required.

Because the charge was so great and the assignment was so heavy, all I could do was attempt to discharge the assignment by faithfully performing the assignment. In other words, I was looking for a place to actualize who I was in God. Even though the time was not right or the season yet ripe, the true me was still present. I came up with my next idea. *Be you within your music group!* I took my new songs and taught them to the group. I also required them to sit through creative Bible studies. The studies were composed from each song's content. And the funny perspective was how the group reacted to the changes. Their reaction gradually became a bowl of comedic frustration.

I watched their faces as I set the weekly agenda. Their irritation became very high, evident in the immediate protests and excessive arguing. It became very obvious to them that rehearsals were becoming more like church services, and they vocalized their displeasure. "You are not our pastor!" and "You're not a minister!" I heard them, but I didn't allow them to detour my passions. In spite of their feedback, I kept teaching. And their love for both the group and me caused them to remain. We had a wonderful team. Overseer was our spiritual leader and I was their musical leader and founder.

This is what I believe Paul, John the Baptist, and other great prophets and apostles experienced when they declared their callings. It's a subjective experience that we spend the rest of our lives attempting to prove objectively. And regardless of their past, the people had to realize it was God who qualifies. God had qualified me to become a minister and even a prophetic leader, so the more I sought God, the more my zeal increased.

And through this new grace, the music possessed a new and improved mission. It now had a different edge. The edge was the emerging prophetic anointing of God! These glimpses of structure and development foreshadowed my apostolic mantle. The apostleship was the last of the words that God had given me through my intense studying, but I was attempting to be those things prematurely and presently inordinately within the wrong environment.

I owe those who were part of the Testify and Divine Compliment era a great level of gratitude. It was through them that I learned how to become a prophet, pastor, teacher, and even the apostle. For that, I am eternally grateful. Knowing what I know now, I wouldn't encourage the emerging prophet to forcibly articulate in a place that is not designed to allow them such a place of prophetic growth. It's imperative that we find our true place of prophetic development. This struggle to find a place of safety to actualize my gift is also part of my puzzle. It was designed for me to go through this grief for God's glory. And being more transparent when I accepted the calling this didn't change my sinful behavior. There were moments of a high propensity of sin, even during my initial days of ministry, and those sinful tendencies were as strong as my spiritual cravings. The seed of addiction, sexual promiscuity, and dishonesty were generational curses within my bloodline.

The confusion of my sinful nature and my sanctification process played critical roles to my aggression in wanting to be something that I was not yet ready or qualified to be. When Samuel anointed David, it was the period of initially recognizing him as king. However, that was the anointing to *become* king, not the anointing to *be* king. David is later anointed king when Saul transitions and the kingdom is ready for his assignment as such. We, too, have to be honest prophets. And we also must be patient with God's process of making us official prophets. For there is a period in the anointing to becoming a prophet, but then there's another anointing of release which is to exercise the fulfillment of our prophetic office. We must be careful that we don't confuse the two.

You may be struggling in your sins and yet still perceiving the call of God upon your life. I want to encourage you. Please stick with God no matter how sticky your situation! We all fall short, but we don't have to remain in our fallen moments. Keep pressing no matter how messed up your life and living may be—regardless of your dysfunctional past, present and even future. Dysfunction will try to override and overtake your life, but your assignment is the key to your survival.

God comes after the heart, not the outer appearance. From my own living, God gave me this prophetic slogan, which I still live and preach to this day. God knows your due date of deliverance. Your demographic, socioeconomic, parental struggle, or dysfunctional history doesn't matter. If God has called, He will continue to justify and purify you. And it is He who has called and chosen all men.

***For the children being not yet born, neither having done any good or evil, that the purpose of God according to election might stand, not of works but of Him that calleth (Romans 9:11).***

The task at hand is to find the right place of spiritual growth. And prophetic growth comes from honesty, sobriety, accuracy, and being under both a suitable and seasoned leader. These tools helped me, and I know they will help you!

## MY PROPHETIC GIFT
**The Revelation of the Band of Prophets and the New Gibeah Ministries for Christ Church**
*1 Samuel 10:5-7*

Psalm 119:105 reads, *Thy word is a lamp unto my feet and a light unto my path*. The long road to sound prophetic awareness and expression has been a series of bumps and bruises, but God's spoken word over my life has systematically brought me to this present station. Simply put, the sixth chapter of Isaiah started my prophetic roadmap to 2 Chronicles 5:11-14. Those verses continued my prophetic roadmap to 1 Samuel 10:5-7. One scripture leads to another, but the vehicle of prophetic validation, within the road that is mapped, is an entirely different matter.

When I noticed the conflict in Testify, I created a new strategy to release my gift and zealousness in other avenues. In August of 2000, I went online to search for a place to share. I found the MSN community site features. The only missing component to my new endeavor was that of a suitable name for the site. During my studies, I remembered the events that shaped the five known prophetic schools of the Old Testament (i.e. *Jericho, Gilgal, Bethel, Ramah and Gibeah*). It was from that study that I extracted the name.

And the last school mentioned became the most impactful to me. For the sequence of the events which takes place, at this place, speaks accurately to my prophetic assignment. That place was Gibeah, which was identical to me. Gibeah is the Hebrew word for "Hill of God" and was both a prophetic and musical place. I later learned that Gibeah was also a Levitical place. It was from this Levitical, prophetic and musical place that I saw my next portal of destiny. Gibeah changed the life of Israel's first king, and from reading this reference, it also changed mine:

**Next, you'll come to Gibeah of God, where there's a Philistine garrison. As you approach the town, you'll run into a bunch of prophets coming down from the shrine, playing harps and tambourines, flutes and drums. And they'll be prophesying. Before you know it, the Spirit of God will come on you and you'll be prophesying right along with them. And you'll be transformed. You'll be a new person! (1 Samuel 10:5-7, the Message Bible).**

"Band of prophets" actually comes from the King James Version of this account. And because it resonated so loudly, I named the online group The Band of Prophets. For the next three years, the Band of Prophets' page would serve as a prophetic metropolis. Anyone needing answers concerning the prophetic could come to this site and I'd teach them. As a result of following my passions, the growth of the site and the growth of my spirit were emerging very parallel. I would hold daily sessions online. I was consumed with teaching and leading God's people in the prophetic while providing strong biblical foundation. The calling of the apostle was coming alive, and during my fasting periods, the Lord informed me that I was an apostle to prophets.

However, the church I was attending was not conducive of me exercising my gift. I was in great conflict. The pastor of the church didn't believe in the apostolic or the prophetic. In spite of this reality, I still felt the tug of my calling. And I felt the urgency to shift from an onsite ministry into an actual church. It was unfortunate that I didn't have the support of my current leader or the proper resources to start, but I kept moving forward. One day, while fasting, the Lord informed me that I would not only father, pastor and be an apostle to prophets, but I would also be called to restore the legitimacy of the prophetic schools.

God said that the prophetic schools would again return to the kingdom. He told me that my assignment was to assist with the defense of the prophetic anointing. I was to bring a greater standard to the gift and the office of the prophet by becoming a prophetic-apostle. What a great call. What Overseer said was making more sense. I certainly wasn't ready back then, but God said it was now time. And with all these prophetic words looming over my head, I decided to share with the members of the online group that I believed God was now calling me to transform the Band of Prophets into an actual church.

I inquired if they were willing to meet for a prophetic symposium and business meeting. Before the meeting, I knew I needed one major addition. Again, I needed a suitable name for the ministry. I strongly felt the name of the community group wasn't enough, so back to my study notes I went. And it was during a fast that the Lord released the vision and ministry name: New Gibeah Ministries for Christ. Not only did He give the name, God gave a clear vision: New Gibeah would be a church filled with apostolic, prophetic and kingdom-minded people. A people who would help create a place for all people to come regardless of color, background, and struggle. New Gibeah is called to be a place where Jesus is the main event. Our church would flow with immense measures of agape love. Out of this scripture, the most important feature came. It was the very mantra for the ministry: *"Strategic Fellowships are Essential to Every Believer's Destiny."*

New Gibeah was envisioned to be a place for people to come and safely encounter God for a heart-changing experience. It would release the power of prophecy as a means of promoting such change. And the authentic worship and genuine fellowship, which is the strategic connection, would serve as the major catalyst of such a divine change.

As a result of this articulation from the Spirit, I wrote the vision down and brought it to those who I thought were ready to run with it. I didn't realize, however, that God had only given just a release to receive the clear vision. For the actualization of the vision is different than its articulation. And in great haste, I attempted to prematurely open the church. In the late summer of 2003, reality came to bite a great chunk out of me. We lasted only a few months because it was not the right time. I had the gift, but I had to get my gift's ability more in order.

It was quite interesting. The 70 souls on the online site turned into a faithful team of 3. The downsizing was an interesting feature that would be a reoccurring theme, even when the church actually reaches its true season of inception. Not everyone will pastor with a large group. Some of us will literally have to be faithful to the smaller numbers. I've also learned that when it's the right season, it doesn't matter how limited your resources are. The unlimited power of God will be the true means of validation. Again, this level of transparency is to assist those young in age and in faith and for those of you who are eager to start a work even now. Let me share this with you. Take your time. Wait on God, for God's day of release is certainly better than yours.

After this period of failure, I reluctantly returned to my former church home for further instruction. This period was another humbling experience. It was relatively a short experience because I didn't fight to humble myself and to be patient in the process. During this time, I was stripped of all positions within the pulpit ministry. My license to preach was revoked, and a brief period of restriction to minister was enforced. But this process of correction was certainly worth the survival of my assignment. And in 2005, after much correction, I would eventually receive proper restoration of license and a formal ordination to eldership.

I was then more equipped to handle the work of the ministry and the office of pastor, but I needed a new leader because the season of my first prophetic mentor was over. Though he and I remained connected, the purpose of connection evolved. I had joined a church and had a pastor even though he was not prophetic. So now I was in need of a pastor, leader and father who could get me back on track to my prophetic assignment. One fall night in 2006, the Lord accomplished that task. I was sitting in a revival on the front row of the church of a childhood friend. The guest speaker came into the sanctuary, looks in my direction and begins to speak in tongues. This was the beginning of my connection with my next prophetic father. And this connection was none other than Dr. Brian J. Mosley. "Prophet" or "Dad" is what I affectionately call him.

For the word of the Lord released from the prophet of God was: "I was a man cut from a different cloth." He also said, "The Lord showed him a large picture that was in the form of a puzzle and it was his assignment to help me piece that puzzle together." As a result of that initial connection and word, I would spend the next two years traveling and training under his ministry. It would be through his tutelage that I would learn what a national and true prophetic father was surely about.

And under his ministry and guidance, I learned the principles for national ministry. After almost three years, in June of 2008, God spoke through the man of God saying that it was time for my release as pastor. He gave me clear instructions, telling me that I would travel to California with one of my group members and upon our return I was to start Bible study. I followed the word of the Lord. When we returned from LA, I opened my home for the first Bible study. It was the last Friday of July and only one person showed up. Despite the size of the Bible study, I instructed as if I was teaching thousands. She listened and supported as if many were present. I must say this: Deaconess Sandra Mikell, I thank God for you still being with me today and for you being able to see what I could see.

We grew to five souls on the official opening of the church and have since grown to seventy members plus and several ministries within the Washington, D.C. metropolitan area. Now the assignment is clearly established. The fulfillment of the work and mantle of the prophet is in a position for proper execution. I know it because I am flowing in it! We now have a legitimate place with a suitable organization to handle God's people. In 2010, I was officially affirmed in the Lord's church as an apostle of the Lord Jesus Christ. This service was conducted by my apostolic father, Bishop Charles Lanier. And now I have all majority of the tools in place. The puzzle is more organized than ever! My church family and adopted family have all united to help me with this vision. It is because of them I am able to carry this vision to the world. And now share this testimony with you.

# 2

# Family

## THE PREMIERE MINISTRY OF GOD:

***These are the generations of the heavens and of the earth when they were created, in the day that the Lord God made the earth and the heavens (Genesis 2:4).***

The prophetic anointing starts with simplicity. And the simplicity of prophecy originates from the storyline of mankind. In fact, Genesis explains everything. Very few people have realized that the journey of the prophet begins with the bloodline of men, by the hand of God. After all, a man of God, is first a man. And man's beginning divulges multiple prophetic connotations and implications, which are also sensible revelations, confirming that the true source of prophecy is a very logical progression. That progression is first taught to us through God's creation of the human race. And reviewing Adam and Eve's storyline, this will usher in more prophetic sobriety. Simultaneously, it will also escort prophetic error to the dry places. For the Holy Writ explains man's creation:

**_And God said, let us make man in our image, after our likeness: and let them have dominion_** **over the fish of the sea, and over the fowl of the air, and over the cattle, and over all the earth, and over every creeping thing that creepeth upon the earth.**

**_So God created man in his own image, in the image of God created He him; male and female created He them._**

**And blessed them, and _God said unto them, be fruitful, and multiply, and replenish the earth, and subdue it, and have dominion_ over the fish of the sea, over the fowl of the air, and over every living thing that moveth upon the earth (Genesis 1:26-28).**

God created the heavens and earth. The writer, who is the Prophet Moses, calls it the Generations of the Heavens and Earth. And on the earlier portion of the sixth day, he releases a remarkable decision. This decision appears as prior thought, a few moments before it's conducted. The conceptualization of mankind is somewhere near the same day of the literal creation of mankind, meaning God preplanned man's creation. The discussion was "let us make him in our image." And yet, the release of his decision is commenced later, but still on the sixth day. God decides to combine eternal power from the heights of heaven, marrying it with temporal plains from the depths of earth. As God works from the great portal of His throne, He creates a composite of His eternal and divine Self.

First, he uses the mist of the ground and the depths of red clay, deep from within the earth. From this combination, a human body is formed. God's portion from the earth is now complete. He then extracts a portion of himself, in addition to a portion of his eternal essence. This essence is better described as eternity, which is better known as Spirit. God's spirit is then released into the nostrils of a lifeless body, and from this divine act of combining earthly and heavenly entity, man becomes a living soul:

**But there went up a mist from the earth, and watered the whole face of the ground. And the Lord God formed man of the dust of the ground, and breathed into his nostrils the breath of life; and man became a living soul. (Genesis 2:6-7, KJV).**

Man is now alive. He's a living, breathing entity walking and living upon the face of the earth. And man is then placed in a location called Eden where God commands man to assume the responsibility of two chief functions: dominion and procreation. Remember these two points, for in them are great prophetic implications. Of the two assignments, one is greater than the other. For the greater of the two is procreation. Man's major assignment is the reproduction of his own similitude. Just as God made the initial replica of His eternal Self from the temporal plains of the depth of earth and those deep realms of His eternal spirit, man has the same power and responsibility. He must multiply and manage what He multiples on top of the environment he is called to oversee.

The resolution of procreation commences when Adam is given Eve. This is why Eve is extracted and created from man to assist man. Every believer accepts Adam and Eve as the first personalities of human life. Everything we learn about them reveals further assistance for all mankind—even the assignment of the prophet, for his creation and purpose upon the face of the earth is intricately wrapped in this foundational truth. This is exhibited many times when referring to the calling of a prophet. When God created Jeremiah, He used this same principle. He took flesh from the creation of new life between a man and a woman and used an extraction of himself by giving a spirit to the prophet and every man.

**Before I formed thee in the belly I knew thee: and before thou camest forth out of the womb I sanctified thee, and I ordained thee a prophet unto the nations (Jeremiah 1:9).**

A prophet is a composite of Adam. He is flesh, soul and spirit. He is an extraction of earth and eternity. He is a combination of ground and God. Just as Adam is a composite of both eternity and earth, the prophet's creation cannot be denied. The dualism of heaven and earth within man is a phenomenon all men are still learning to engage. This is why God places certain abilities and responsibilities within man for man's furtherance and growth; God's chief pleasure of creating man starts with this initial impartation. The very first man and woman are assigned to procreate and to dominate the earth. From their initial procreation, they have placed these same abilities and various traits within us.

Together, they are instructed to produce the highest creation known to the earth! This organism is called the human family. The definition of the human family is the expansion of mankind. The expansions of mankind are mere extensions of this first family. We call these extensions children. It is the presence of children which substantiates a human civilization, which perpetuates the greatest of all systems. Again, that system is the FAMILY! This is an important word, even for prophecy.

Family is the premiere ministry of God. It is the combination of ground and God, as well as that of earth and eternity! And regardless of conditions or circumstances, one thing is for certain: God has given man the power to produce and reproduce. Man wants and possesses this innate desire to see more of his image. This is a very natural rite, but it is also a very supernatural prerogative. It is the assignment of man to make more of him for the glory of God. Surprisingly it is permissible to do so at drastic and alarming rates. In other words, man can duplicate as much as he wants. This is divine right and divine power from Adam unto all men.

This seems like narcissism, but is instead a divine principle extracted from creationism. This principle is called the law of duplication. We simply say: Be fruitful and multiply. And the law of human duplication is the only means whereby a true process of the human family can truly emerge. Anything else outside of this concept should be labeled an abomination. Naturally speaking, unless natural birth or adoptive measures are taken, a reconstruction of the first family outside of these properties is surely illegal. Man was for woman and woman helped produce the family. The family is the chief structure that even God still operates spiritually and naturally therein.

And the fruitfulness of the production of a family is the highest honor a family can provide God. Being fruitful and multiplying is not a condition of being out of order! In fact, it shows there is much order when this is properly done. Israel was even hated for their ability to reproduce at such expeditious and exponential rates:

**And the children of Israel were fruitful, and increased abundantly, and multiplied, and waxed exceeding mighty; and the land was filled with them. Now there arose up a new king over Egypt, which knew not Joseph. And he said unto his people, behold, the people of the children of Israel are more and mightier than we: Come on, let us deal wisely with them; lest they multiply, and it come to pass, that, when there falleth out any war, they join also unto our enemies, and fight against us, and so get them up out of the land.**

**Therefore they did set over them taskmasters to afflict them with their burdens. And they built for Pharaoh treasure cities, Pithom and Ramses. But the more they afflicted them the more they multiplied and grew. And they were grieved because of the children of Israel (Exodus 1:7-12)**

Multiplication doesn't come without challenges and conflicts. Not only are there demonic assassinations, there are also demonic abominations. Abominations and assaults have been attacking the human family ever since the beginning of all families. One major abomination is the presence of sin. When sin enters the world, a drastic presence aggressively interferes and undermines the fullest potential of the family. This presence is none other than the enemy of all souls: the devil. As a result of sin's entrance, the first family followed the devil's deception, and mankind received an irreversible verdict:

**Wherefore, as by one man sin entered into the world, and death by sin; and so death passed upon all men, for that all have sinned (Romans 5:12, KJV)**

The verdict is a limitation of life. Because of sin, there is a shorter period of time for each man to live. And Satan is the culprit and the agent; sin is his accomplice. Sin now works with another entity, incrementally removing man from the portal of this world. The extraction process which removes him is the process of the spirit called death:

**And unto Adam he said, because thou hast hearkened unto the voice of thy wife, and hast eaten of the tree, of which I commanded thee, saying, thou shalt not eat of it: cursed is the ground for thy sake; in sorrow shalt thou eat of it all the days of thy life; thorns and thistles shall it bring forth to thee; and thou shalt eat the herb of the field; in the sweat of thy face shalt thou eat bread, till thou return unto the ground; for out of it wast thou taken: for dust thou art, and unto dust shalt thou return (Genesis 3:17-19, KJV).**

Man's reality originally was supposed to be eternal. Never did God want a temporal presence, but as the result of sin, Satan and the fall of mankind, death now enters the reigns of men's lives. Death permeates the earth's regions, causing the unfortunate decline of man's image from his true image. Sin also diminishes the essence of eternity, making the spirit of man dead. Nonetheless, that image is still a composite of the glory of God—even in the midst of this present gloom.

For man still ascertains the supreme privilege of procreation power. Because He is still made in the image of God, this provides him a connection to unlimited potential. The image of God still silhouettes near the image of man, but unfortunately, man can only generate lower grades and composites of an even lesser replica of himself. Man is still permitted the same power to produce and reproduce. However, he can only accomplish this assignment with a more diminished capacity. That doesn't mean, however, that his assignment is over.

It means that through this error, God allows man to keep the grace upon his life. Man is obligated to operate within the primary callings: procreation and limited realms of dominion. Man is still called to make the first ministry, the family. And man must continue to walk worthy of his vocation, regardless of his present condition or the reality of his dysfunctional capacities. Forging the assignment of the family is still of the utmost importance. For the assignment of the family is the premiere ministry of God.

## THE ASSIGNMENT OF MANKIND IS THROUGH THE CONDUIT OF GENERATIONS

As families expand, so does the conceptualization and classification of the family. God has created a channel of classifying families through the conduit called generations. The word generation is from the verb "generate." It is synonymous with the word procreate. Therefore, to generate (or procreate) means to bring something already in existence, further into existence.

When a man brings forth a legitimate family of a wife and children, he is bringing into existence his immediate generation. And all the positions within the immediate generation are equally as important. A generation is properly composed of founding patriarch (a father) and matriarch (a mother). The father and mother unite and create ordinate offspring, naming them sons and daughters. This is the construct of an immediate family.

Each cascading cluster of subsequent generations further creates superimposed positions within the family of that given generation. This is how we get the presence of the positions of great-grand parents and grandparents. It even presents uncles, aunts, cousins, and in-laws.

When God dealt with the children of Israel in the area of severe punishment, God explained that the duration of his punishment usually last until the fourth generation (Exodus

20:5). This implies how a generation's responsibility is to communally and properly produce until it reaches its fourth generation, whereby a new cycle within that family's generation can occur. And once a family reaches a true cycle of its fourth generation, then that generation recycles to the first generation. Adam was the beginning of the first conduits of the generations of all mankind:

**<u>This is the book of the generations of Adam</u>. In the day that God created man, in the likeness of God made he him; male and female created he them: and blessed them, <u>and called their name Adam</u>, in the day when they were created. And Adam lived a hundred and thirty years, <u>and begat a son in his own likeness, after his image;</u> and called his name Seth (Genesis 5:1-3, KJV).**

The phrase "and called their name Adam" simply can be understood as Adam's generation being called "the Adamic Generation." As we see here, Adam reproduces replicas of himself when he reaches age 137. His newest son, Seth, is considered a newer version of his father, Adam. Seth is the next generation of Adams. And when Seth reaches the age of maturity, he then becomes responsible for the next creation of his own generation.

Studying biblical generations, you will learn how each has its own unique quality and assignment. Instead of naming him the second Adam, he is named Seth for a greater reason. Seth's name comes with a meaning and its own divine identity. This identity is solely based on his generational assignment. The Hebrew meaning of the name Seth is *substitute*. It is the generation of Seth that becomes the substitute generation for the lost generation of Abel. As we know, Abel is brutally murdered by Cain. And Cain, Abel and Seth, are all the children of Adam. The three mentioned sons are all of the Adamic Generation.

## **ASSIGNMENTS AND DEADLINES**

From Abel's birth, his gifts and talents were for the purpose of tilling the ground. Abel was gifted in the art of agriculture, so if Seth is born as a literal replacement of Abel, it is quite clear that Abel's destroyed destiny by Cain is now Seth's assignment. For it is Seth who literally replaces Abel's life and his work by taking on his gift and assignment of agriculture.

This substitution within the generation of Adam was one of the first passing of mantles. Like Elijah does with Elisha, Moses does with Joshua, Jesus does with his apostles, and now his apostles have done unto us, mantles can be transferred through generations or through adoptive means within a generation. This also teaches how Abel's generation survives and now lives on within the generation of Seth. It is through Seth's generations that the advancements of the art of agriculture will increase to aid mankind's food consumption within the earth. And Abel's life, through Seth is still possible only because of the act of procreation with Adam and Eve's creation of Seth preserving Abel's generation.

We have to see our assignments more deeply than we've ever seen them before. The major goal within the assignment of each family (or each family's ministry as I like to call it) is the unique purpose for which God creates each family. Adam successfully does his. Cain and Abel had theirs. Then Seth took on Abel's because Abel was not permitted to finish it. So the work within the Adamic Generation shows the importance of fulfilling your assignment by demonstrating why we must accomplish this with every urgent realization; there is an unknown amount of time for each man to accomplish his assignment. We are now reminded and made aware. Mankind is within a limited currency of time to produce generations. Not only is he sent to produce his generation. He must find out the unique purpose of his generation. That is why we must understand we are on a time-sensitive matter, and it is of utmost importance that man becomes more aggressive concerning this urgency.

Some men have dual responsibility. If he or she is a man or woman of God then there is a natural and supernatural assignment of birthing two distinct generations. For their distinct generations will help subsequently produce natural and spiritual generations to come. So we must remember: Time is not on our side. And God makes this very clear. Mankind has lost portions of the essence of eternity within the earth realm. His once glorified flesh is certainly condemned and destined for unfortunate return to the earth. And his spirit lies dormant and dead without any further perception of God. And his soul is displaced, surely in need of redemption and deliverance. These are the consequential verdicts rendered because of the depravity of sin. And the ramifications of such actions speak strongly about divine judgment:

**And the Lord said, my spirit shall not always strive with man, for that he also is flesh: yet his days shall be a hundred and twenty years (Genesis 6:3, KJV).**

***The days of our years are threescore years and ten; and if by reason of strength they be fourscore years, yet is their strength labor and sorrow; for it is soon cut off and we fly away (Psalm 90:10).***

Adam and his subsequent children lived a very long time, but they still faced death. God gradually declines mankind's lifespan. In one era, it was a guarantee of 120 years. By the days of this particular psalmist, there is now a possible guarantee of 70 years. The maximum promise was for some to even reach eighty years. So man only has a certain amount of time to fulfill his responsibility of creating and duplicating images of his once divine, and yet diminished self. Each family's assignment of their own continuation and extension is now temporal instead of eternal. This is why it is imperative that man is properly birthed, developed and released to complete the deadlines on his assignment. Jesus tells us plainly how this works.

***I must work the works of him that sent me, while it is day: the night cometh, when no man can work (John 9:4).***

For the night, in the proverbial sense, means death. And when death occurs, whatever project or purpose one's participating therein, there is no more allotment for contribution and time. Death—which can be abrupt, violent and even sudden—finishes it. Most don't know when death is coming, so it's important that we are focused and become fervent in our assignments. The prophet has an assignment. The prophet has a generational assignment. The prophet has a family into which he belongs, and it's important that the prophet finds home because time is of the essence.

## OPERATION URGENCY: FROM GENERATION TO GENERATION

*One generation passeth away, and another generation cometh: but the earth abideth forever (Ecclesiastes 1:4).*

Each generation has a limited timeframe to produce and manifest the next generation. For each generation, God has decided to bring forth a specific purpose within the earth. Like a factory line producing cargo, they are to increase and release whatever gifts and talents God has given. This natural calling is a divine blessing and ability which is a means of service (i.e. ministry) for the earth. But remember, it has been given with an unknown and divinely allotted period of time. This is also true for the spiritual prospective of producing spiritual sons and daughters.

Even though man is on a limited time schedule, God will not retract the abilities of man. In spite of a stifled divine nature within man there is still a remnant within the DNA of mankind that God wants continually reproduced. The urgency is now! The generational assignment to make the next generation is certainly now. Each generation must become connected to the Adamic assignment which is to be fruitful and multiply. When Jesus teaches the lesson of the talents, this very lesson echoes this urgent mandate:

*And unto one he gave five talents, to another two, and to another one; to every man according to his several ability; and straightway took his journey. Then he that had received the five talents went and traded with the same, and made them other five talents. And likewise he that had received two, he also gained other two. (Matthew 25:15-17, KJV).*

When this lesson begins to close, we see that there is one more person given the same responsibility (Matthew 25:18). Yet, the amount given to him was the smallest of all sizes mentioned. His disobedience of not fulfilling the law of multiplication surely becomes his greatest consequence:

**And so he that had received five talents came and brought other five talents, saying, Lord, thou deliverdest unto me five talents: behold, I have gained beside them five talents more...He also that had received two talents came and said, Lord, thou deliveredst unto me two talents: behold, I have gained two other talents beside them....Then he which had received the one talent came and said, Lord, I knew thee that thou art a hard man, reaping where thou hast not sown, and gathering where thou hast not strewed: and I was afraid, and went and hid thy talent in the earth: lo, there thou hast that is thine. His lord answered and said unto him, thou wicked and slothful servant, thou knewest that I reap where I sowed not, and gathered where I have not strewed...Take therefore the talent from him, and give it unto him which hath ten talents...And cast ye the unprofitable servant into outer darkness: there shall be weeping and gnashing of teeth (Matthew 25:20, 22, 24-28, 30, KJV).**

This explains a universal law about God's assignment for each generation: God wants increase. The same is expected with respects to those assigned to the spiritual component. Spiritual fathers and mothers are no different than natural parents and the concept of procreation is very similar to the parable of these three given each a certain amount to multiply. Just as a woman's natural biological clock is ticking, so does the spiritual makeup of a natural or spiritual parent tick within themselves of such an annoying urgency. They know within themselves that they have a limited, unknown amount of time. They know that they are called to gather the spiritual family as well as the natural family. They are hardwired to continue to produce and reproduce the Spirit's generations of God unto Jesus Christ. This is a natural and supernatural assignment and urgency.

Jesus Christ had this same concept in mind. He knew his time of earthly ministry wasn't for very long. He was on a tight schedule, so he produced twelve sons who we call apostles. These apostles, minus one, grew into 120 souls. Those 120 souls became 3,120 souls. Overtime, the generations of Jesus Christ have become billions. The fruitfulness started with the first spiritual generation of these eleven apostles. They were fruitful and multiplied without any excuses!

Certainly, this was regardless of the shape of the man and the assignment of the generation. Each apostle emerged in his gifts and talents, which was all part of God's plan. The Bible makes this very clear. There are perfect gifts flowing within imperfect people:

**Every good gift and every perfect gift is from above, and cometh down from the Father of lights, with whom is no variableness, neither shadow of turning (James 1:17, KJV)**

We also now know that we don't need repentance to accept callings and gifts:

***For the gifts and calling of God are without repentance (Romans 11:29, KJV)***

So all generations must emerge! And all families come forth! For Men and women of God; natural and supernatural parents are all responsible for procreating more in natural and the Spirit realms! And it's time to produce the prophetic sons of God. Simply put: Just as Adam and Eve's family were created to do something more than existent, so are each of our natural and spiritual families. The Apostle Paul teaches, that we are earth and spirit with treasure inside of us:

***But we have this treasure in earthen vessels, that the excellency of the power may be of God, and not of us (2 Corinthians 4:7, KJV).***

Therefore, it is the responsibility of the progenitor of each generation to impart such training of their ascertained skills to their next generation. This is how God works naturally and supernaturally within each generation. It is his means of achieving the advancements of mankind and also create further glorification of His eternal Self. With this understanding, the supernatural family must now embrace their unique and spiritual destiny:

***Mark ye well her bulwarks, consider her palaces; that ye may tell it to the generation following (Psalm 48:13).***

***This shall be written for the generation to come: and the people which shall be created shall praise the Lord (Psalm 102:18).***

So the assignment of man is within his current generation. His assignment is bigger than his time. It is about preserving the work and seed of the generation by imparting into the next generation. Every man has this assignment. And every generation of the Bible records their assignment for us to follow as our chief example.

*Apostle Sherman D. Farmer*

## THE REVELATIONS ABOUT MEN IS THROUGH THE CONDUIT OF GENEALOGIES:

The flow of generations and the contributions of each generation can be found within the listings of most biblical generations. These listing are seen in the books of Exodus, Numbers, Chronicles, Matthew, and Luke. These listings are what we call "genealogies." When reading about biblically recorded generations, certainly there is a greater call to practice the interpreting of such anomalies.

Most people bypass them altogether, and the average Christian oftentimes overlooks such features when reading scripture. Looking at the phrases such as "one who begets another" can seem somewhat boring, but the interesting prospective of viewing biblical genealogies isn't any different than researching your own family tree. Jesus says every big and small thing must be fulfilled from the word of God. This means even the exclamations, punctuations and overlooked situations (like genealogies) are not to be taken lightly:

***For verily I say unto you, Till the heaven and earth pass, one jot or one title shall in no wise pass from the law, till all be fulfilled (Matthew 5:18).***

Every inkling will be prophetically confirmed. And each small matter will expand into a greater understanding. For these minute matters will also speak louder and even clearer before

God returns. The genealogies of the Bible seals the history of man, and they also reveal God's deeper plans for mankind. The gradual loudness of the genealogies will emphatically speak more than just a list of men begetting men. For when reading genealogies, we can also discover prophetic purpose within them.

The etymology of the word *genealogy* comes from the word *generation*. And biblical genealogies are designed to show the proper flow of each man's family and bloodline. Therefore, the purpose of a genealogy helps with the maintenance of history within each biblical family. The genealogies of Adam show us the founding fathers; the genealogy of Levi shows the priests and temple leaders; the genealogy of Judah shows the kings which led to the ultimate king of kings, Jesus Christ. This is why genealogies are very important; it is high time to stop overlooking them. For in them contains the conduits that reveal greater revelations about men.

And even though daughters and mothers are rarely mentioned, they too are just as important. Regardless of the primary mentioning of fathers and sons, each son and daughter of the founding parents to their corresponding generation are evidence or gathered DNA between the founding parents for a unique reason. They are assistance to their generations. When watching consistent growth through genealogies, the discoveries are limitless.

Genealogies are divinely sent to help us learn something more through the Holy Spirit. And if we continue to overlook the richness of revelations within them, we will experience continual danger and penalty of the sin of omission:

***All scripture is given by inspiration of God, and is profitable for doctrine, for reproof, for correction, for instruction in righteousness (2 Timothy 3:16, KJV).***

The greatest revelation that genealogies provide is the confirmation of each biblical family's assignment. You can logistically tract the family of farmers, musicians, priests, and kings by watching the emergence of each generation within their own genealogy. How does this parallel with the prophetic? There is an original genesis for all generation of prophets. There is a biblical founding prophetic family which produces the creation of all prophetic generations. These prophetic generations can be confirmed by the genealogies of their generations. And there is a genetic gene placed in a certain family who is solely responsible for the production of prophets. Like the movie *The X-Men* which talks about mutants who are gifted with a certain gene, the gift of prophecy is both genetic and generational. And the functionality of a prophetic family is very similar to the makeup of the natural family.

**<u>Heed this prophetic word: True Balance will restore to the prophetic gift when we disciple prophetic families after the Adamic paradigm.</u>**

A father is a father by its truest definition. It doesn't matter what type of adjective is placed in front of the assignment of father. A father is a father as long as he has a son. When speaking about spiritual fathers, with modern-day kingdom practices, the principles of spiritual fathering often goes haywire.

Paul, the Apostle is a great example of a modern day spiritual father. He was very detailed in the shaping of his sons. And Timothy was well developed for ministry by the time his pastor and spiritual father released him into full time ministry. Nowadays, we have men proclaiming their spiritual fatherhood but with a lack of molding.

The same way a natural father's absence is a consequence of many men's identity, is the same conflict which causes many prophets to have mishaps in ministry. And the great pretending of the so-called spiritual fathers make this divine role seem like a big joke.

We have made this subject matter so abstract that the best solution is to return to the original context of the natural assignment of fatherhood. Whether speaking on fathering, parenting, children, or family, a natural correlation is the best pattern to assume. Just like a father talks with his son; spends time helping his son into becoming a man, we need spiritual fathers to be more hands on with their spiritual emerging sons. This principle is the same with that of a prophetic father. We need more prophetic fathers willing to train up new prophetic sons.

For a prophetic father isn't any different than Adam. Adam is the father of fathers. Similarly, a prophetic father is the father of prophets; prophetic fathers seek to create prophetic sons just as Adam did with his own three sons. And the truly legitimate prophetic fathers are not creating sons because of some secret motive of narcissism. Yes true spiritual fathers are not dissociative to the cause of spiritual parenting. A prophetic father is sent to create and shape his unique prophetic family.

He is also sent to create a prophetic environment for his family. Therein resides his true purpose which is to populate the kingdom with suitable prophetic children. As you can see, there is no difference between God's assignment for Adam and Eve, Christ and the church, and a prophetic father and son. All of this comes from watching the genealogical trends of biblical generations.

And what a wonderful construct God has given. This is the reason a prophet can represent God on earth—because he is a particle from Adam's generation. In Adam is God and earth combined. The prophet's assignment is to work in the earth for God. Therein reveals the genesis of the prophet's purpose. He is certainly like Adam: temporal because earth is in him and eternal because God is speaking through him.

So we shouldn't be so quick to overlook Adam! And we certainly should stop avoiding the journey into generations and genealogies. These organizational charts are divinely written and released by the Spirit of God with equal importance, just as the biblical narratives and doctrines.

Again, there are former prophetic generations, genealogies, families, and fathers! The evolution of a prophetic family originates from God, who strategically creates a natural family of prophets. And the visibility of their generations and genealogies are spread within major moments of Israelite history. It is from personal study that God has allowed this discovery of that certain genealogy which reveals the generation of prophets who were responsible for the continuation of the prophetic anointing.

These prophetic genealogies are still relevant in today's church. As the Bible declares, the foundation of the church is established on the ministry of the prophets and apostles (Ephesians 2:20). If our foundation is based on the prophets and their evolution, then it behooves us to intently look therein. For the ministry of the family is not a natural assignment alone. In other words, there are greater implications of the purposes in the spirit realm for the existence and creation of the natural and conventional family.

After all, the first church is not the New Testament church. It's the church of blood relatives who are called the church of the wilderness (Acts 7:38, KJV). And in the scheme of this same design, it is our assignment to follow the patterns already prescribed. Family is the first ministry and if a ministry is operating like a family, then there is a better cohesiveness and proper flow of spirituality.

And family provides the basic necessities of life. Food, clothing and shelter are all part of these amenities. And so it is the same in the spirit. Spiritual children need spiritual food so that they may grow and become strong. Spiritual children need proper clothing, which is called in "the biblical sense" the receiving of a mantle. This mantle will cover them in their travels within the world of ministry and Christianity. And spiritual children need a home to grow until they have become grown whereby they are challenged and charged to create their own family. The same way we raise a natural family. We must raise a prophetic family and its subsequent generations.

Therefore, we will intricately study the prophetic generations and genealogies in order to learn prophetic government, community and accountability. For the genealogies of the generations of the prophetic family of the Bible reveals how to be a more effective prophet unto the children of men and the people of God.

**APOSTOLIC REVELATION**

- The portion of man that comes from the earth is being called back to the earth.

- The portion of man that is from heaven is being called back to heaven.

- The essence of man's abilities and talents (that are within him) are being called to the next generations (after him).

- Children born into a certain generation are divinely placed into that generation for the acquisition of each generation's specific traits, skills and abilities. They are children of their corresponding parents and former parents from previous generations for this very reason.

A child cannot deny its DNA, no matter the lot of the family. It is the child's responsibility to accept their family and their generational assignment. For as man has the natural assignment of self-procreation of a natural generation, the spiritual family has the assignment of procreation in the supernatural.

It is the same with those born through the Spirit and received into the Spirit of Adoption of their given prophetic family. A prophet's succession is just as important as an apostolic succession. The prophet is sent by God through Christ, by way of the Spirit, into their destiny and assignment which only can be achieved by finding the proper conduit of generation and genealogy that God has assigned them to operate therein.

# 3

# From Levi to Jesus

## PROPHETIC GENERATIONS; GENEALOGIES AND GOSPELS

### The 1st Generation: Levi
*The Prophetic Patriarch of the Prophetic Generations*

---
Levi establishes fellowship and relationship
for the family of prophets

---

***And she conceived again, and bare a son; and said, now this time will my husband be joined unto me, because I have born him three sons: therefore was his name called Levi. (Genesis 29:34).***

There is a specific assignment for every prophetic family, even the prophetic families of this dispensation and time. The first assignment of learning about the generations starts with formation; origins provide assistance to this beginning. The visibility of order can be seen in biblical generations and genealogies, and there is a great connection and correlation of their revelation within the Gospels.

The first four prophetic generations of the Bible produces a foundational understanding that there should be other prophetic generations in the Bible and within the modern world. Adam and Eve serve as the genesis for our first parents. Equally, there are prophetic parents who serve as the origin for the beginnings of the prophetic family. Their roadmap begins with Levi and continues with Jesus Christ. But it does not end with Jesus Christ. The prophetic generation continues with me and you.

Biblically speaking, the prophetic family's revelation starts with Jacob. For Jacob and Leah are the founding parents of the first prophetic generation. Jacob unknowingly gives this gene to Levi who becomes the pre-patriarchal carrier of the largest and most formidable of all prophetic generations. The prophetic gene is on a deliberate journey and with a specified deposit. That journey is conducted solely by God: first with Jacob, who inherited from his grandfather Abraham, who inherited from his forefather Enoch. As we can see, the generation of Adam to Shem connects the flow of this gene and its assignment.

We must clearly understand the prophetic mantles of Enoch, Abraham and Jacob (Jude 14; Genesis 20:7; Genesis 49). The prophetic begins with Enoch. He is of the seventh generation of Adam. Prior to Enoch, there was no prophetic person or presence. After Enoch is taken from the earth and Noah's sons are born, the prophetic gene doesn't appear again until Abraham. After Abraham, there is a brief interval of the prophetic gene during the days of Isaac, but the gene to prophesy is still within the blood line of this particular family. Its next emergence takes place with Jacob.

We witness this when Jacob prophesied at the end of his life. Jacob arose from his deathbed to prophesy the future and destiny of his twelve sons. One of his sons was none other than Levi. Levi travels into Egypt with his father and his children (when Joseph is discovered to be alive). He lived for a period of 137 years before dying (Exodus 6:16b). The age of 137 is the same age Adam was when he and Eve produced Seth (Genesis 5:3). What great irony! The word given by his father speaks volumes to his destiny of becoming the next prophetic carrier to God's people:

**Simeon and Levi are brethren; instruments of cruelty are in their habitations. O my soul come not thou into their secret; unto their assembly, mine honor, be not thou united: for in their anger they slew a man, and in their selfwill they digged down a wall. Cursed be their anger, for it was fierce; and their wrath, for it was cruel: I will divide them in Jacob, and scatter them in Israel (Genesis 49:5-7)**

For their insubordination of murdering the man that raped their sister, Simeon and Levi would forever be known by their ability to mutilate and murder. This became their chief representation and assignment. Jacob's prophecy was accurately confirmed. Levi's purpose wasn't solely prophesy. However, his descendants were to become priests and servants of the sanctuary. They continually had to mutilate and murder. This death process was performed daily during animal sacrifices made in the tabernacle and temple rituals. It was also the reason Levi didn't inherit any land within Canaan. His people were distributed within every tribe of his brothers.

The descendants of Levi were assigned to keep charge of the tabernacle and faithfully serve within the house of God. During the days of the wilderness journeys, their additional responsibility was the carrying, transporting, erecting, and dismantling of the portable and massive tabernacle. In the days of the Promised Land, they continued their Levitical and Priestly assignment with designated offices within the temple. The work of the Levite and the priest was a major stewardship. Their entire family had to minister to millions, but their presence was still the symbol of great worship. And even now a unique model is associated in the blending of Christianity as a Jewish priesthood (1 Peter 2:9).

A prophet's job is to connect people to God, and this was the chief embodiment of Levi's name and purpose. The etymology of Levi's name means to *be joined,* which is another way of saying fellowship. Levi's Levitical and priestly assignments were foundational assignments of joining other descendants of God with God. And Levi's existence can now be considered as the first of the four initial prophetic generations. Thus, Levi's presence created the beginning of all prophetic generations.

## The 2nd Generation: Kohath
*The Second Prophetic Generation's Patriarch*

---

Kohath continues the establishment of assembling the family and ministry of the prophets

---

***And the sons of Levi, Gershon, Kohath and Merari (Genesis 46:11)***

Levi and his wife produced three children. Three seems to be a prevailing number among Levitical realities. Levi is the third born of his father and mother and produced three sons with his wife. Three is the number of divine and earthly agreement (Amos 3:3; 1 John 5:7). The numeric presence among Levi and his father's sons continued with the amount of sons he was given. The number three becomes the solidified number representing the Levitical worship team and experiences of Israel. And the Levitical paradigm also became the foundational format within the first family of prophets (see the next chapter).

A momentary breaking of this monotony occurred when God chose the next chosen son of Levi. Instead of God choosing the third or firstborn, he chose Levi's second born, Kohath. This is not a deliberate transfer, but was orchestrated by God. We are simply following the generations and genealogies to gain further understanding of God's momentum to the prophetic anointing within their family. It is therefore imperative that we don't attempt to manipulate this gene or this gift.

The storyline of Kohath is very vague. When Jacob and his sons moved to Egypt because of God's preserving power through Joseph, Kohath was born prior to this experience. Kohath lived for a period of 133 years (Exodus 6:18), and it is very likely that he was present when his grandfather prophesied before dying on his deathbed. Little did he know he would inherit such a great gift. Not much is spoken of him directly, but much is said about him through his lineage.

Amongst his four children, sacred Levitical responsibilities were accepted and assumed. The first responsibility was the sole possession of the priesthood (1 Chronicles 23:12-13). All of Aarons' descendants became the generation for the priesthood of Israel. During the Wilderness Journey Periods, Kohath's descendants became attendants of the innermost sacred possessions of the tabernacle (Numbers 3:27-32; Numbers 4:1-20).

The Ark of the Covenant, Table of Presence, and the other artifacts of the Holy of holies were their responsibility to bear. While the other sons of Levi were given wagons and oxen to assist with their loads, Kohath's children had to carry these items on their backs (Numbers 7:9). This implication of heavy service implies a great accuracy of accountability required by the hands of the Kohathites.

Kohath's children are not just priestly, but they are also Levitical. The center of the tabernacle and temple's prophetic music ministries would be led by Kohath's sons (1 Chronicles 6:31-38). David employed 120 of Kohath's descendants when he finally managed to bring the Ark of the Covenant into Jerusalem (1 Chronicles 15:5). David would also organize the prophetic temple singers and musicians from all Levitical families, but chiefly from Kohath's family (1 Chronicles 23:3-6).

A famous Levitical and prophetic singer, Heman was a descendent of Kohath (Heman was Izhar's son, who was Kohath's second born son and Heman's ancestral forefather). Heman and his family of 14 sons and 3 daughters become another large family of prophetic, musical and Levitical singers. They were chief musicians and worshippers during the days of David and Solomon (1 Chronicles 25:4-5). The family lineage of singers continues throughout the days of the kings: 2 Chronicles 20:19-28.

**But not all Kohathites were reliable in ministry. There are a few who are infamous for their erring presence:**

1) **Nadab and Abihu**
   (Two of the sons of Aaron, who are also Amram's grandchildren & Kohath's great-grandchildren) offered strange fire before the Lord and were dramatically put to death by God: Numbers 3:4 (Leviticus 10:1; Numbers 26:61; 1 Chronicles 24:2)

2) **Korah**
   (The son of Izhar, who is Kohath's second born and Kohath's grandfather) caused a revolt among the congregation and was also penalized with death for his insurrection: Numbers 16

**We have many famous prophets who are born directly within the Kohathite bloodline:**

- **The Prophet Samuel** (Descendent of Izhar – Kohath's second born) – 1 Chronicles 6:28 (1 Chronicles 6:22)

- **The Prophet Jeremiah** (Descendent of Amram – Kohath's first born) – Jeremiah 1:1 (1 Chronicles 6:60)

- **The Prophet Ezekiel**
  (Descendent of Amram – Kohath's first born) – Ezekiel 1:3

- **Zechariah**
  (Descendent of Amram – Kohath's first born) – Zechariah 1:1 (Nehemiah 12:4, 16 – Iddo is of the priestly line therefore he is a Kohathite)

The presence and name of Kohath and any descendent becomes synonymous with a high measure of service, skillful musicality, the greatest of Levitical responsibilities, and a fluidity among the prophetic family and ministry paradigm. The etymology of the name Kohath means *assembly*. Thus, Kohath's generation becomes responsible for further assembling the family and ministry of prophets.

## The 3rd Generation: Amram (Jochebed)
The Third Prophetic Generation's Patriarch & Matriarch

---
Amram and Jochebed forerun the highly graced prophetic family.

---

*"...And Kohath begat Amram"* **(Numbers 26:58b)**

***And Amram took him Jochebed his father's sister to wife: and she bare him Aaron and Moses: and the years of the life of Amram were a hundred and thirty and seven years (Exodus 6:20, KJV).***

In Levi's next generation, Kohath produced four sons (1 Chronicle 6:1). Among Kohath's four sons, Amram is the one chosen to carry the prophetic gene further into his family line. Amram was the firstborn of Kohath. The Bible declared that Amram married Jochebed. From this union, a *powerful shift* occurs within the prophetic family.

Levi's wife was not mentioned by name anywhere in scripture. This is very standard among genealogies. However, rare exception is made with the mentioning of Kohath's wife. The reason being is not because of who she birthed, but her true relation to whom she married. The connection of Jochebed and Kohath produced a very poignant perspective among the Kohathite family.

This connection created the continued use of Kohath's name. It also becomes the epitome of classifying anyone or any group who is truly prophetic. This storyline was so poignant that it impacted my life drastically. The very name Kohath is now categorized as the name of our church's prophetic presbytery and school, the Assembly of Kohath. Again this stems from Jochebed and Amram's heavy connection.

The text makes the connection very clear. Amram, who is Kohath's firstborn, and Jochebed, who is Kohath's baby sister is the cause of God lingering the importance concerning the name of Kohath. Notice the pericope. It says **'his father's sister' (Numbers 26:58)**. And another passage reverses their first source of connection:

**"And the name of Amram's wife was Jochebed, the daughter of Levi whom her mother bare to Levi in Egypt..." (Numbers 26:59a)**

Amram married his father's sister. Jochebed is also Amram's grandfather's daughter. So if Jochebed is Kohath's sister and Levi's granddaughter, this would make Jochebed Amram's aunt (before she became his wife). Jochebed's generational placement sustains the continuation of the second generation. She is the confirmation of that generation alongside her brother, Kohath's firstborn son. She married into the third generation of Kohath when she married Amram. Two plus three equals five which is the number for grace, so grace is mingled within the crossbreeding of two Levitical generations.

**"Amram married his aunt Jochebed..." (Message Bible)**

Another important observation is her age. Jochebed's age is implied when mentioning the location of her birth (Numbers 26:59). Jochebed's three older brothers (Gershon, Kohath and Merari) were certainly born prior to Egypt. Other than this information, nothing more is provided in the scriptures concerning Amram except that the etymology of his name is *people of the highest*. And the etymology of Jochebed's name is *Jehovah is gracious*. The combination of their name can mean the highest people who are receiving the graciousness of God. This subjective interpretation of the combined names can symbolically relate to the next generation of Levi. It would be that pending generation who became the symbol of the Kohathite name and the prophetic family. For God was soon to release the highest people of the Levitical family who are the most graced of all prophetic families.

## The 4th Generation: Moses (Mariam and Aaron)
*The Fourth Generation's Patriarch of the First Biblically Recorded Prophetic Family*

Moses, Aaron and Miriam become the First Family of Prophets

***And the name of Amram's wife was Jochebed, the daughter of Levi, whom her mother bare to Levi in Egypt: <u>and she bare unto Amram Aaron and Moses, and Miriam his sister</u> (Numbers 26:59, KJV).***

The prevailing number of three returns again to Levi. The next generation produced three children and from the union of Amram and Jochebed, the birthing of the fourth prophetic generation emerges. This generation is the one we've been waiting for! It is the highest prophetic people graced by God. Miriam was their firstborn and only daughter of the three. Aaron was the firstborn son and middle child, and Moses was their youngest and final son. God would bypass the first and second and use Moses, the third born of the fourth generation. Moses would restore the balance of the prevailing number of three within the Levitical reality. He would also become the first prophetic general of all prophetic families.

The fourth generation released the first prophetic family paradigm. And the marriage of Amram and Jochebed released a special grace to produce this fourth generation. Grace comingled with this crossbreeding makes Moses, Aaron and Miriam the prophetic byproduct of Levi's prophetic children. Their presence alone substantiates a family oriented and prophetic environment. Each prophetic member of this first prophetic family can be legitimately confirmed as a prophet by scripture.

## Further Confirmation of the First Prophetic Family

### THE RULING-(GOVERNMENT) PROPHET: MOSES

Moses is the under-shepherd of the Old Testament church of the wilderness (Acts 7:38, KJV). He is the younger of two other siblings, but is still God's chosen leader of the three prophets:

*And Moses was fourscore years old, and Aaron was fourscore and three years old, when they spake unto Pharaoh (Exodus 7:7).*

During the time of Pharaoh's massacre of male Israelite newborns, Miriam must have been of a reasonable certain age when her mother used her to assist with saving Moses from Pharaoh's plot of annihilation. Jochebed hides Moses as long as she could before she takes and places him in an ark of bulrushes, while his sister watches him travel upstream from afar:

*And there went a man of the house of Levi, and took to wife a daughter of Levi. And the woman conceived, and bare a son: and when she saw him that he was a goodly child, she hid him three months. And when she could no longer hide him, she took for him an ark of bulrushes, and daubed it with slime and with pitch, and put the child therein: and she laid it in the flags by the river's brink. And his sister stood afar off, to wit what would be done to him. (Exodus 2:1-4).*

This also explains Aaron's age again. Pharaoh was murdering all infants up to a year of age. Aaron was three years old and Miriam was most likely between 10 to 12 years of age. In spite of Miriam's age and Aaron being the firstborn male child, and both being prophetic, it was God's will for Moses to be their prophetic leader:

**And there arose not a prophet since in Israel like unto Moses, whom the Lord knew face to face, in all the signs and the wonders, which the Lord sent him to do in the land of Egypt to Pharaoh, and to all his servants, and to all his land (Deuteronomy 34:10).**

Moses is the greatest prophet of all time within the era of the Old Testament. He is the first leading prophet of the family type prophetic guild. This prophetic guild is composed of a nucleus of his brother, sister and himself. Moses's position teaches the importance of having a prophetic leader. God's predestinated plan graces one with the anointing to prophetically lead other teams of prophets (i.e., Samuel, Elijah, Elisha, and even Paul the Apostle). Therefore, Moses being chosen was not a matter of popularity or image, but was a matter of the supreme election of God. And Moses is the symbol of the leading and fathering prophet.

## THE ADMINISTRATIVE-(SERVING) PROPHET: AARON

Aaron's prophetic ability is very unique compared to Moses's. The Bible doesn't denote how long he or Miriam prophetically flows, but it does provide indication of their specific prophetic unction. Aaron apparently was gifted in public speaking rather than singing or music. Therefore, he served more in an administrative capacity for Moses. He was a prophet to his brother by being the spokesmen of God proxy of his brother. Aaron's assignment was to interpersonally flow between Moses, Pharaoh and the leaders of Israel. This is why Aaron's prophetic position only came about because of Moses's reluctance in leadership:

**And the anger of the Lord was kindled against Moses, and he said, Is not Aaron the Levite thy brother? I know that he can speak well. And also, behold, he cometh forth to meet thee: and when he seeth thee, he will be glad in his heart. And thou shalt speak unto him, and put words in his mouth; and I will be with thy mouth, and with his mouth, and will teach you what ye shall do. And he shall be thy spokesman unto the people: and he shall be, even he shall be to thee instead of a mouth, and thou shalt be to him instead of God....And the Lord said to Aaron, go into the wilderness to meet Moses. And he went and met him in the mount of God, and kissed him. And Moses told Aaron all the words of the Lord who had sent him, and all the signs which he had commanded him. And Moses and Aaron went and gathered together all the elders of the children of Israel: and Aaron spake all the words which the Lord had spoken unto Moses, and did the signs in the sight of the people. (Exodus 4:14-16, 27-30).**

**And the Lord said unto Moses, see I have made thee a god to Pharaoh: and Aaron thy brother shall be thy prophet (Exodus 7:1)**

Aaron's prophetic ability shifts from being the representative of Moses and the people to the priestly position as the oracle of God. He was made High Priest over all Israel. His greater assignment was to stand before the holy of holies and continue his prophetic and priestly assignment before God on the behalf of the people. He was called to speak proxy on the behalf of them in the most sacred space only once a year on the Day of Atonement.

Aaron's prophetic ability was not positioned in front like Moses's or Miriam's. Rather it is an internal anointing for the interpersonal relationships of Israel's between God and his people. He speaks as both a senior counselor and oracle of God. Aaron's position is the symbol of the servant prophet.

## THE INSPIRATIONAL-(CHARISMATIC) PROPHET: MIRIAM

Miriam is mentioned specifically in the fourth generation even though she isn't listed in all biblical genealogies (see Exodus 6:20). Additional information concerning Miriam's birth and Levitical connection is seen in certain passages of scripture. Her position within the family is big sister, but amongst the congregation of Israel, she was called a prophetess. Her unique anointing for leading worship and women is exemplified on the day of deliverance at the Red Sea. She is also gifted with the art of music and singing like her younger brother, Moses:

***Then sang Moses and the children of Israel this song unto the Lord...And Miriam the prophetess, the sister of Aaron, took a timbrel in her hand; and all the women went out after her with timbrels and with dances (Exodus 15:1a,22, KJV).***

Miriam is the only female prophet of the first prophetic team. Females are not normally mentioned within genealogies, and a chauvinistic group would suggest she possibly was a subordinate prophetic leader. However, a prophet can be a leader within a spiritual body regardless of gender (Galatians 3:24). And Prophet Micah confirms that Miriam's legitimacy as a leading prophet is valid:

***For I brought thee up out of the land of Egypt, and redeemed thee out of the house of servants; and I sent before thee Moses, Aaron, and Miriam. (Micah 6:4).***

## Conclusion of the First Prophetic Family

In 2 Corinthians 13: 1, Paul declares "in the mouth of two or three witnesses every word be established." God sent three prophetic voices to establish not only a major movement of deliverance, but also a distinct formation of prophetic demonstration. The corporate demonstration of this prophetic family confirms the need for the return of the prophetic family. And the confirmation of Amram and Jochebed's children, as **prophets, are clearly seen within Scripture.**

*"And the children of Amram; <u>Aaron, and Moses, and Miriam</u> ...." (1 Chronicles 5:2a)*

This guild is composed of a complete generation of siblings who are bonafide blood relatives from an immediate family. The 4th generation of Levi is called to lead the people by prophesying as a leadership team. Each prophet is called to operate within their own unique grace. Moses leads, Aaron administrates, and Miriam assists the women and worship. Yet they remain functional intact as a spiritual and natural family.

Their natural family roles are incrementally suspended while functioning as Israel's spiritual leaders of God. Naturally speaking, Moses should have followed Miriam or even Aaron. Typically, younger siblings are trained to follow the oldest, but God turned this paradigm the other way around. And we can only imagine how idiosyncrasies of this reality challenged their mentalities. We see this during their certain errors. For instance, when Miriam was punished for insubordination (Numbers 12), and when Aaron failed by being easily manipulated by the people during the Gold Calf incident (Exodus 32). Not to mention the possible bond between Aaron and Miriam was stronger than what they each had with Moses due to the late interaction among them. For Moses spent majority of his life in the palace of Egypt. This needful separation for the plan of God doesn't negate the social dynamic's impairment of missing childhood connection and adulthood growth together. This could have possibly caused Moses to feel brief moments of awkwardness and alienation.

But the challenges did not change their assignment. They were siblings, but the senior siblings did not outweigh God's decision in using the youngest. And regardless of their age, the three prophets served as a synergy from God. Together, they produced a strong prophetic flow and force while governing the entire nation. It would be advisable to classify Israel as the first of mega-churches. Moses, Aaron and Miriam were prophetic pastors united and as a corporate ministry of prophets. Their presence reaffirms the need of the return to the prophetic family paradigm, which is currently a missing commodity. It would bring a better balance to the prophetic purposes of God. I strongly believe that God wants this paradigm to return within the body of Christ. As the scripture shares with us, there is nothing new under the sun. And within each rotation of the sun, the ministry of the prophets can and will return:

***I have also spoken by the prophets, and I have multiplied visions, and used similtudes, by the ministry of the***

***prophets (Hosea 12:10).***

Nine is the symbol of spiritual birth and the symbol of the Holy Ghost (i.e. there are nine fruits of the spirit as referenced in Galatians 5:22-23). And when you add up each of the referenced generations' natural birth, you have this same number. Levi was third born, Kohath was second born, Amram was firstborn, and Moses was third born. When all four orders of birth are added, the sum is nine.

**This Apostolic Revelation decrees and declares:**

**God wants the return of Prophetic Guilds' and Prophetic Families. And true prophetic fruit is accomplished when the true prophetic generations will manifest and maintain throughout the remaining generations of the earth.**

**The Lord says, it is time to give birth to the next and newest prophetic generation! And because of Jesus' connection to this generation we have an even firmer foundation to this revelation.**

## The Return of the Kohathite Anointing: John, the Baptist (Zechariah)

*"...He shall purify the sons of Levi, and purge them as gold and silver, that they may offer unto the Lord an offering in righteousness. Then shall the offering of Judah and Jerusalem be pleasant unto the Lord, as in the days of old, and as in former years"* **(Malachi 3:3b-4, KJV).**

Over a period of time, the assignment of Levi becomes polluted and distorted. This even coincides with the ministry and families of biblical prophets. God promised purification among the Sons of Levi, and the purification process He promised finally came. Levi's purification began with the formal release of John the Baptist. It is John's father, Zecharias, who is also a Kohathite from the priestly lineage of Aaron who ignited this process. And when God releases Zecharias from a lengthy silence, his prophetic anointing released on the day of John's birth (Luke 1:67-76).

Theologians unanimously ascribe the fulfillment of the prophecy of Malachi during these beginning moments within John's ministry. They also agree that John was the greatest prophet to have lived. His life seemingly swung like a pendulum between the portals of both testaments. Even Jesus stated how John was greater than any other prophet and more specifically how he was more than just a mere prophet (Matthew 11:1-14). It is because John got to see what Old Testament prophets could only dream about. He got to see Jesus Christ! But there is a greater irony to this storyline and it goes back to Levi and Kohath:

**There was in the days of Herod, the king of Judea, a certain priest named Zecharias, of the course of Abia: and his wife was of the daughters of Aaron, and her name was Elisabeth (Luke 1:5, KJV).**

John and his parents are from the same Kohathite family line as Moses, Miriam, Aaron, and even Samuel, Heman, Ezekiel, Jeremiah, and Zechariah. This connection alone makes John Levitical, priestly and prophetic. And we clearly discover his origins through the slight genealogy mentioned in Luke's gospel (i.e. Abia,or Abijah as referenced in1 Chronicles 24:10). Priest Abijah was a descent of Aaron which indicates that he was also a descendent of Kohath. And every descendent of Kohath is a prime candidate for the prophetic anointing.

## The New Kohathite Generation: Jesus Christ

*"The book of the generation of Jesus Christ..." (Matthew 1:1a, KJV)*

The sealing of the purification process of Levi began with John the Baptist and his father. Finalization was through the manifestation of the ministry of Jesus Christ. Jesus's ministry was subsequent of John. It was Jesus who sealed Levitical and prophetic reformation. Further studying of genealogies, generation and the gospel reveals how John and Jesus are in fact blood cousins. Elizabeth is called a daughter of Aaron (Luke 1:5b). And Mary, Jesus's mother, is directly described as Elisabeth's cousin. This immediate kinship is a major confirmation to Jesus Christ being Judean and Levitical:

**And, behold, thy cousin Elisabeth, she hath also conceived a son in her old age: and this is the sixth month with her, who was called barren (Luke 1:36, KJV).**

Collectively, Jesus, John, and their ministries purified Levi and revived the purpose of the family of prophets. Like Aaron, Jesus was also called the supreme High Priest. It was prophesied that the Messiah would equally become prophet, priest and King:

**And the multitude said, This is Jesus the prophet of Nazareth of Galilee (Matthew 21:11)**

***Now of the things which we have spoken this is the sum: We have such a high priest, who is set on the right hand of the throne of the Majesty of heavens (Hebrews 8:1, KJV).***

We who accept Jesus as Lord, through the gift of salvation and the Holy Spirit become candidates for the gift and office of prophecy. Not only because we have the Spirit of Christ, but because we also have the blood of Jesus upon us and spiritually within us. And this blood is the source of the true bloodline of Levi and prophetic anointing. Once we have received the gift of the Holy Spirit, a prophetic release can occur, but this assignment must be taken on with accurate understanding. True prophetic anointing can only begin with Jesus Christ. He is the father and source of prophesy. From Enoch, Abraham, Jacob, Levi, Amram, Kohath and all of his descendants unto us, there has to be a legal and logical connection. The means of legal connection can only be obtained by becoming part of Israel's family. And the only way into the first family of scripture is through salvation in Jesus Christ.

If a sign of prophetic flow is solely based on a believer's positioning within Christ's household then we must become part of the family of Jesus Christ, the prophetic patriarch of this generation and master prophet of all true prophetic houses. And into his spiritual family is the first connection any emerging prophet must pledge:

***But Christ as a son over his own house; whose house are we, if we hold fast the confidence and the rejoicing of the hope firm unto the end. (Hebrews 3:6, KJV).***

The prophetic gene Jesus passed from the Generations of Adam, Shem culminated with himself. He is our second Adam and second Moses. His assignment as the second Adam was to restore obedience to the generations of mankind. His assignment as the second Moses was to provide a spiritual exodus from the bondage of the Egypt of sin and the ruler ship of the Satanic-like representation of being a pharaoh who no longer knew God. Just as God visited the third and fourth generations, he also did so within every third and fourth generational assignments of Jesus Christ.

*Apostle Sherman D. Farmer*

## The Cycle of the New Generational Deliverance

The Bible teaches that God heavily moves within bloodlines by every third and fourth generation. It's in the fourth generation that God guarantees a finalization to whatever judgments, blessings, curses, and deliverances has taken place.

This divine concept is revealed as God administered the Ten Commandments:

***Thou shalt not bow down thyself to them, nor serve them: for I the Lord thy God am a jealous God, visiting the iniquity of the fathers upon the children unto the third and fourth generation of them that hate me* (Exodus 20:5 – See also: Exodus 34:7, Numbers 14:18, and Deuteronomy 5:9].**

When God told Abraham that Israel would be in Egypt for a period of 400 years, he also informed Abraham about Israel's due date of deliverance which preset at God's appointed time. This appointed time is parallel to the presence of Israel's fourth generation.

***But in the fourth generation they shall come hither again: for the iniquity of the Amorites is not yet full* (Genesis 15:16).**

When God rewarded Jehu for cleansing the land of its wickedness, He rewarded a generational blessing for Jehu. This generational blessing was the continuity and posterity of kingship among Jehu's descendants. God promised Jehu that four generations of kings would come from his bloodline:

***And the Lord said unto Jehu, because thou hast done well in executing that which is right in mine eyes, and hast done unto the house of Ahab according to all that was in mine heart, thy children of the fourth generation shall sit on the throne of Israel (2 Kings 10:30).***

The word of the Lord concerning Jehu's lineage certainly came to pass:

***This was the word of the Lord which he spake unto Jehu, saying, thy sons shall sit on the throne of Israel unto the fourth generation. aND SO IT CAME TO PASS. (2 Kings 15:12)***

Rewards, breakthroughs, judgment, consequences and deliverances last by generations. God always honors and never falls short of His word! And when the fulfillment of the fourth generation occurs, the cycle renews and the new generation becomes the first within that family's lineage. They are called to complete a whole new cycle of purpose within their family.

Jesus Christ was called to bring continuity and posterity to the perpetuation of the prophetic anointing. If this is the case with John and Jesus; Elizabeth, Zecharias and Mary, then we have, yet again, witnessed the power of God's word fulfilled... Zecharias, Elizabeth and Mary symbolize the third generation of Kohath, while John and Jesus symbolize the fourth.

We are now called to reproduce more prophetic generations for the congregations of the body of Jesus Christ. We too have an assignment within the household of faith which is to produce the legitimate return and institution of this first prophetic family structure from God. When this is done, then our prophetic brothers, sisters and children can advance. Thus becoming better in God, for the workings of God, by building subsequent prophetic generations to come:

**For He established a testimony in Jacob, and appointed a law in Israel, which He commanded our fathers, that they should make them known to their children: That the generation to come might know them, even the children which should be born: who should arise and declare them to their children: That they might set their hope in God, and not forget the works of God, but keep His commandments (Psalm 78:5-7).**

Saints of God, The Lord is building a testimony in each of us, just as He did with Jacob, Levi and His Kohathite sons. God also appointed this specific word among His people. For He now desires to use the presence of current New Testament prophets within the church who must develop and then deposit the revelations and fundamental of old and new into their prophetic children:

**Tell ye your children of it, and let your children tell their children and their children another generation (Joel 1:3).**

Therefore, it is the next generation's responsibility to create prophetic houses in order to continue working this important assignment. This assignment is from God through Jesus Christ who has given prophets the supernatural power to fulfill this prophetic mandate continually within the earth. And we are to work diligently until the Lord Himself is pleased and says this assignment is complete within perspective generations.

But God is not finished with this purpose nor is He finished with the prophet or his presence. As prophets of God within the true prophetic family of God, we have Levitical, Priestly and a prophetic responsibility to uphold our prophetic lineage and pedigree. We are to do this by and under the name of Jesus Christ. Whereas, all roads led to Levi and then Jesus, they are now pointing to us.

# 4

# Capitals & Diasporas

## THE RELEVANCE AND REVELATION OF CAPITALS AND DIASPORAS

### The First Capital of Humanity
*The Edenic Environment*

Every natural family is designed to abide in a certain place of residence as a means of fostering and facilitating the furtherance of their family life. Usually, those places throughout scripture are termed territories, lands, lots or inheritances. More importantly, these particular places are given special names to indicate their specific importance. The founding family, Adam and Eve, were designed to abide in a specific dwelling place. It appears that this place, Eden, is where God wanted the entire world to be governed.

Eden was the first capital and civilization recorded in scripture, even though its citizens were very few. When researching the definitions of the name Eden, we discover that it means *pleasure or pleasantness*. Thus, Eden was a place of pleasure—not only for agriculture and animal life, but it was a place of pleasantness because the first family of mankind dwelled therein.

**"...The Lord God planted a garden eastward in Eden; and there he put the man whom he had formed" (Genesis 2:8, KJV).**

**"...And let them have dominion over the fish of the sea, and over the fowl of the air, and over the cattle, and over all the earth, and over every creeping thing that creepeth upon the earth...and God blessed them, and God said unto them, be fruitful, and multiply, and replenish the earth, and subdue it: and have dominion over the fish of the sea, and over the fowl of the air, and over every living thing that moveth upon the earth. (Genesis 1:26b, 28, KJV).**

All major decisions and influences by the first family were accomplished from this assigned location. The first assignment of the first family was procreation; the second was dominion. This is why Eden is considered a capital. It was a capital based on its purposes and those who resided in it (Adam and Eve). Another very important purpose of Eden was Adam's generations are supposed to have lived eternally within Eden:

**And the Lord God took the man and put him into the Garden of Eden to dress it and to keep it (Genesis 2:15, KJV).**

When Adam and Eve erred in their sin, the consequences affected their demographic, physical and spiritual make up. The physical consequence was Adam and Eve being removed from

Eden and having the gift of eternal life retracted from them. Their spirits then died, their souls became bound for hell, and their flesh were condemned to return back into the earth. Their dejection was a form of protection. God did not want Adam and Eve eating from the tree of life which would have perpetuated their sinful state, so the verdict was eviction. As the result of their expulsion, this is how we understand scripture's first diaspora.

## The First Diaspora of Humanity
### The Adamic Generation

***Therefore the Lord God sent him forth from the Garden of Eden, to till the ground from whence he was taken (Genesis 3:23, KJV).***

A diaspora is the process of voluntarily or involuntary removal from a person's original location of birth and ancestral origin. African Americans are the result of a slave trade diaspora, which was an involuntary experience. And now their presence has become global. All people of African descent around the world can trace their ancestry back to Africa. And the same is applicable of the people of Jewish descent. From Egypt to Palestine, and from the period of the Holocaust until now, the Jewish are attempting to return to Israel, their original source of ancestral origin.

Adam and Eve's family experienced an involuntary diaspora because of their sin in the Garden of Eden. Their judgment was done with a forcible move while Cherubim stood guard with a flaming sword. Adam is made to become a severe worker of the very environment that he was partially made from. He was assigned to till the earth until he returned to the earth. And this judgment is still in effect until mankind experiences the fullness of redemption and restoration of his essence called eternity.

Even though the first family of mankind erred, there is still a continued responsibility for every person within the Adamic Generation to accomplish their specific assignment. They are to accomplish this regardless of their present location and spiritual predicament. We clearly see that even in judgment and the result of the diaspora, mankind still produced successful experiences. The first successful experience was Cain's development of his own generations and civilizations. It was Cain who successfully left the confines of his mother, father and Eden to create his own civilization:

**And Cain went out from the presence of the Lord, and dwelt in the land of Nod, on the east of Eden (Genesis 2:16, KJV).**

Away from his parents, Cain set out to find a place to live and create the future generations of his own family. This is the assignment of all families whether they reside in their place of origin or are of a diaspora. They too are to find their own place in the world. Within that place, they are to effectively carry out their continued responsibility of the survival of their family.

The assignment is still operative as long as the individual is alive to pursue their assignment.

Regardless of situations, each generation has to have a location that they can term their spiritual capital. Until they find their spiritual capital, they have to work within their spiritual diaspora. The Bible shares how Cain migrated and maintained. Even Adam and his other family members were obedient to that call, regardless of the absence of Eden. However great the challenge presented by their new environment or proximity, man must complete their overall assignment. The producing of subsequent generations can be fulfilled anywhere.

Regardless of the division of their specialty, each of Adam's sons belonged to his bloodline. And each son had the same responsibility as their father in conjunction with their own unique ability. For example, Cain was called to be a shepherd and herdsman, but his overall assignment was procreation and thus the creation of his own subsequent generations. Cain subdued the earth as an Adamic descendent by taking on the talent of being gifted with shepherding. Cain also creates, builds and names a new place as the capital of his civilization. The uniqueness of the naming is because it is the name given after the birthing of his first born son:

**And Cain knew his wife: and she conceived, and bare Enoch: <u>and he built a city, and called the name of the city, after the name of his son, Enoch</u>. (Genesis 4:17, KJV).**

The meaning of the city is based on the meaning of his son's name. Enoch's name means *dedicated*. It was a place dedicated to the existence of his family and thus his people. Therefore, Cain and his children continued the assignments of their father within their own capital. The city of Enoch was not only a place for the generations of Cain, but it became a place where many great skills and talents emerged from the subsequent generations of Cain's bloodline:

**And unto Enoch was born Irad: and Irad begat Mehujael: and Mehujael begat Lamech. And Lamech took unto him two wives: the name of the one was Adah, and the name of the other Zillah. And Adah bare Jabal: he <u>was the father of such as dwell in tents, and of such as have cattle</u>. And his brother's name was Jubal: <u>he was the father of all such as handle the harp and organ</u>. And Zillah, she also bare Tubal-Cain, <u>an instructor of every artificer in brass and iron</u>: and the sister of Tubal-Cain was Naamah. (Genesis 4:18—23)**

This text further implies how Cain was possibly a type of governmental leader because he was the founding forefather of his own county. Cain built his own civilization from the creation of his own generations.

## **_And the deeper revelation is the emergence of the generations of the family:_**

As his children were born and became of certain age, each exhibited their own unique abilities. It is my belief that these abilities are provided by God, unto man and through man, as a means to help govern their new capital.

- Jubal (one of Cain's descendent) was gifted as the originator (or father) of music. Jabal (another descendent of Cain) was gifted to govern agriculture and cultivate farm life (similar to Cain, their founding forefather).
- And Tubal-cain (another Cainite descendent) was talented and skilled in the artistry of using brass and iron for various creations of vessels and weaponry. – Genesis 4:20-23

This confirms that within each generational bloodline of the human existence there will be an emergence of unique creativities for a specific assignment within each given family. Some families will be created to birth and produce artists, scientists, carpenters, scholars, architects, government leaders, etc. It's all based on the forefather and the assigned capital to accomplish such tasks. Likewise, this reality is validated in the supernatural and spiritual realms. Some families will be birthed to create a prophetic generation and prophetic families for generations to come. As in this case we discovered Levi was the descendent designated with this responsibility. And Levi also experiences his very own Levitical Diaspora.

*Apostle Sherman D. Farmer*

## The Genesis of Levitical Diasporas

The diaspora of Levi's emergence starts with the DNA of Levi. Levi's character shapes his destiny. For Levi was known to be impulsive and aggressive; he was a man very driven towards violence and fighting, being attracted to blood and death. It looks like a few strands of Cain manifested through him. After all, Cain, Levi and Jacob are offspring of Adam. And when we often think of a Levite in the metaphorical sense, we have no idea how Levi's DNA is an assignment of one who loves to take life.

Levi's behavior and nature echoes the backdrop to the purpose of God's cultivation of his destiny. Levi's descendants were destined to become those who would have to assist with the slaughter of animal sacrifices for the entire nation of Israel on a daily basis. But in order to understand the purpose of the Levitical diaspora, Levi's genesis of error must be revisited.

Out of twelve sons between Jacob with his two wives and two concubines, a daughter was also born. Her name was Dinah. Dinah one day went sightseeing without any male supervision. As a result of this unwise decision, she was cornered by a man who took advantage of her. Hamor of Shechem raped her and then fell in love with her.

She was violated and taken without proper ritual and permission. When her brothers returned from the field after watching their father's cattle, they heard the news. Simeon and Levi became fueled with anger. Their plan was to exact revenge. Not only did they kill Hamor, but they slew the entire city:

**And it came to pass on the third day, when they were sore, that two of the sons of Jacob, Simeon and Levi, Dinah's brethren, took each man his sword, and came upon the city boldly, and slew all the males. (Genesis 34:25, KJV).**

After the massive slaughter, they returned to their family. And Jacob, their father, shows great disapproval. He also expresses his concern and fear of retaliation. Jacob saw their actions as a cause for bringing great reaction among the surrounding civilizations within the land of Canaan. He attempted to maneuver low and off the radar. He didn't want to bother any nation because he realized that his family was too small to undergo such potential attacks, but Levi's revenge on the behalf of his sister causes Jacob's concerns to arise. Jacob grew highly fearful for his small and defenseless family.

**And Jacob said to Simeon and Levi, ye have troubled me to make me to stink among the inhabitants of the land, among the Canaanites and the Perizzites: and I being few in number, they shall gather themselves together against me, and slay me; and I shall be destroyed, I and my house. (Genesis 34:30, KJV).**

When Levi heard his father's response, it didn't concern him as much as the integrity and honor of his sister's name being taken from him. It appeared that Levi's aggression got the best of him (Genesis 34:31). Herein resides the beginning story of Levi's willingness to slaughter.

On another occasion, during the Golden Calf incident, Moses was on the mountaintop receiving instructions from the Lord. Aaron was manipulated into following the people's command.

The issue of Moses being up in the mountain for the length of time is what made the people pressure Aaron into taking some of the gold given to them from Egypt to build the calf. So Aaron created a Golden Calf for idolatrous worship. When Moses returned, he strongly rebuked them for their inappropriate behavior. Residing faithfully among and apart from the congregation were now the children of Levi. When Aaron constructed the calf, they instinctively knew not to follow Aaron's act. Moses saw this as an opportunity to set order. The next act was still congruent to their forefather's act concerning his sister Dinah. For Levi's descendants were used to slay all false worshippers on that very day:

**Then Moses stood in the gate of the camp, and said, who is on the Lord's side? Let him come unto me. And all the sons of Levi gathered themselves together unto him. And he said unto them, thus saith the Lord God of Israel, put every man his sword by his side, and go in and out from gate to gate throughout the camp, and slay every man his brother, and every man his companion, and every man his neighbor. And the children of Levi did according to the word of Moses: and there fell of the people that day about three thousand men. (Exodus 32:25-28, KJV).**

It is from these accounts of scripture that we gain a clear picture of Levi's personality, temperament, and destiny. As we notice the same temperament in Levi is also seen within his subsequent generations. The sons of Levi have a talent and a taste for taking life. He and his children were not afraid to use a knife. As Jacob prepared to die, he made it clear what he foresaw within the destiny of Levi. It was from Jacob's own prophecy that we see the preparation for Levi's diaspora. As a result of Levi's action with Simeon, Jacob calls Levi a murderous man and an instrument of cruelty:

***And Jacob called unto his sons, and said, gather yourselves together, that I may tell you that which shall befall you in the last days. Gather yourselves together, and hear, ye sons of Jacob; and hearken unto Israel your father….Simeon and Levi are brethren; instruments of cruelty are in their habitations. On my soul come not thou into their secret; unto their assembly, mine honor be not thou united: for in their anger they slew a man and in their selfwill they digged down a wall. Cursed be their anger, for it was fierce; and their wrath, for it was cruel: I will divide them in Jacob, and scatter them in Israel. (Genesis 49:1-2, 5-7, KJV).***

But the plot to Levi's destiny surely thickens. God not only saw the bloodthirstiness of Levi. He also saw the greater usage of the life of Levi's descendants. God created a system of worship and sacrifice. And Levi would play an intricate part in this extraordinary design.

## Levi – The Human Tithe for God:

*And the Lord spake unto Moses, saying, And I, behold, I have taken the Levites from among the children of Israel instead of all the firstborn that openeth the matrix among the children of Israel: therefore the Levites shall be mine; Because all the firstborn are mine; for on the day that I smote all the firstborn in the land of Egypt I hallowed unto me all the firstborn in Israel, both man and beast: mine shall they be: I am the Lord (Numbers 3:11-13).*

Like Adam and Eve were expelled from their destiny of having one specified place allotted to them, Levi was also destined to be scattered like random seeds among all the other sons of Jacob. The sons of Levi were destined to become scattered as a sign of Jacob's distress and God's judgment concerning their founding father's actions. But their sense of loyalty to God was also rewarded.

The scattering of Levi was not just a form of punishment for the sin of their forefather murdering the man who raped his sister. But Levi becomes a form of payment unto God to cover the cost of delivering the children of Israel from Egypt. The release of the death angel on all the firstborn males of Egypt was compensated in God's very act of wanting a tribe of firstborns from Israel. When Israel finally arrived in Mount Sinai, God explained his mandate of firstborn males and even cattle. However, he decided to use the tribe of Levi as his designated choice.

The Israelites and the Levites were separately numbered during this moment at Mt. Sinai. Levi's three sons produced astounding populations. The oldest, Gershon: 7,500; Kohath, the second born: 8,600; and Merari, the youngest: 6,200. Making the total amount of Levites a grand total of 22,000 souls who were God's payment (Numbers 3:39). Levi became God's human tithe to himself.

But the amount of other Israelites was 22, 273 (Numbers 3:43). God came up with a payment system for the extra 273 males. This monetary donation was collected by Moses and given to Aaron (Numbers 3:48-51). God was very specific. He wanted fair payment for each Israelite child born and preserved, and for each Egyptian child who died. Even though Israel's sons were larger than Levi's, the taxes of the tabernacle would be payment enough. And the 273 additional males were paid for through the system that is now called the shekel of the sanctuary (Numbers 3:46-47). This system is the beginning of the tradition of the temple taxes.

The collection of Levi went even further when God brought Israel into Canaan by the ministry of Joshua. Through Joshua's leadership, the proper distribution of the land to the other eleven tribes of Israel was provided. Each son of Israel received their territory except for Levi. Again, Levi was the tithe of God. As a sign of God's tithe, the sons of Levi were strategically scattered within each corresponding territory and tribe of their father's brothers:

**And the Lord spake unto Aaron, thou shalt have no inheritance in their land, neither shalt thou have any part among them: I am thy part and thine inheritance among**

*the children of Israel. And, behold, I have given the children of Levi all the tenth in Israel for an inheritance, for their service they serve, even the service of the tabernacle of the congregation (Numbers 18:20-21)*

*Wherefore Levi hath no part nor inheritance with his brethren; the Lord is his inheritance, according as the Lord thy God promised him (Deuteronomy 10:9)*

*"Only unto the tribe of Levi He gave none inheritance; the sacrifices of the Lord God of Israel made by fire are their inheritance, as He said unto them....But unto the tribe of Levi Moses gave not any inheritance; the Lord God of Israel was their substance, as He said unto them" (Joshua 13:14, 33)*

*"But the Levites have no part among you; for the priesthood of the Lord is their inheritance..." (Joshua 18:7a).*

Levi's destiny was clear. It was a form of punishment and payment. Levi received a place to stay in each land, but it was not theirs. Within their allocation of certain cities and suburbs, these places become Levitical capitals. God strategically scattered the generations of Levi by allotment of each patriarchal father of Israel. And each Levitical family was placed in each founding father's territory:

| Tribe Territory Distribution | |
|---|---|
| **Merari** | Reuben, Zebulun, Gad |
| **Kohath** | Simeon, Judah, Dan, Benjamin, Joseph (Ephraim & ½ Manasseh) |
| **Gershon** | Asher, Issachar, Naphtali, Joseph (½ Manasseh) |

The children of Merari and Gershon were logistically distributed by the size of their sons. Each (Numbers 3:18) and Merari (Numbers 3:20) had two sons, but the primary focus was Kohath. Kohath produced four sons (Numbers 3:19). And of all Levitical Families, Kohath was the main family that received the most territory.

- Gershon, the oldest Levitical-forefather, received territory in 3 and ½ tribes.

- Merari, the youngest Levitical-forefather, received territory within 3 tribes.

- Kohath received territory within 4 and ½ tribes.

**Notwithstanding the land shall be divided by lot: according to the names of the tribes of their fathers they shall inherit. According to the lot shall the possession thereof be divided between many and few. And these are they that were numbered of the Levites after their families: of Gershon, the family of the Gershonites: of Kohath, the family of the Kohathites: of Merari, the family of the Merarites. These are the families of the Levities: the family of the Libnites, the family of the Hebronites, the family of the Mahlites, the family of the Mushites, the family of the Korahites. And Kohath begat Amram. And the name of Amram's wife was Jochebed, the daughter of Levi, whom her mother bare to Levi in Egypt: and she bare unto Amram Aaron and Moses, and Miriam their sister...And those that were numbered of them were twenty and three thousand, all males from a month old and upward: for they were not numbered among the children of Israel, because there was no inheritance**

given them among the children of Israel (Numbers 26:55-59, 62).

Now these are their dwelling places throughout their castles in their coasts, of <u>the sons of Aaron, of the families of the Kohathites</u>: for theirs was the lot. And they gave them Hebron in <u>the land of Judah</u>, and the suburbs thereof round about it....And to <u>the sons of Aaron they gave the cities of Judah</u>, namely, Hebron, the city of refuge, and Libnah with her suburbs, and Jattir, and Eshtemoa, with their suburbs. And Ashan with her suburbs and Beth-shemesh with her suburbs. <u>And out of the tribe of Benjamin</u> Geba with her suburbs, and Alemoth with her suburbs, and Anathoth with her suburbs. All their cities throughout their families were <u>thirteen cities</u>. <u>And unto the sons of Kohath which were left of the family of that tribe</u>, were cities given out of the half tribe, namely, out of <u>the half tribe of Manasseh</u>, by lot<u>, ten cities</u>...and <u>the residue of the families of the sons of Kohath</u> had cities of their coasts out of <u>the tribe of Ephraim</u>. And they gave unto them, of the cities of refuge, Schechem in mount Ephraim with her suburbs: they gave also Gezer with her suburbs, and Jokmeam with her suburbs, and Beth-horon with her suburbs. And Aijalon with her suburbs, and Gath-rimmon with her suburbs: and out of <u>the half of the tribe of Manasseh:</u> Aner with her suburbs, and Bileam with her suburbs, for the family of <u>the remnant of the sons of Kohath</u>. (1 Chronicles 6:54-55, 57-61, 66-70).

## Further Study of the Kohathite Diaspora:

Kohath received 23 cities from 6 out of 12 tribes of Israel. There are five (Joseph's sons accounts for two, whereby making it six) tribes responsible for housing Kohathite families. It is in those territories that our prophetic capitals are birthed:

- **Judah**
- **Benjamin**
- **Simeon**
- **Dan**
- **Ephraim (Joseph)**
- **Manasseh (Joseph)**

*And the lot came out for the families of the Kohathites: and the children of Aaron the priest, which were of the Levites, had by lot out of the tribe of Judah, and out of the tribe of Simeon, and out of the tribe of Benjamin, thirteen cities (Joshua 21:4)*

*And the rest of the children of Kohath had by lot out of the families of the tribe of Ephraim, and out of the tribe of Dan, and out of the half tribe of Manasseh, ten cities (Joshua 21:5)*

Six territories (or tribes) received remnants of the Kohathite diaspora. Thirteen cities belonged to Aaron's descendants (the priestly side of Kohath). And the additional supportive tribes of Kohath (Miriam, Moses, Kohath's other three other sons Izhar,

Hebron and Uzziel as referred to in 1 Chronicles 6:2) children would receive the remaining balance of 10 cities. The Kohathite distribution is divided equally into three cities (for Kohathite priests) and three cities for the supportive Kohathite tribes:

- The three Tribes who gave to the Kohathite Priests: Simeon, Benjamin and Judah

- The three Tribes who gave to the Remaining Kohathite Levites: Dan, Ephraim, and ½ of Manasseh

Not every tribe mention released the same amount of cities. It's important to know the cities' correlation to the tribe because it helps when the tracing of lineage begins. Majority of the known prophets of scripture should be able to trace their lineage to either Kohathite origin or a priestly Kohathite origin:

**All the cities of the children of Aaron, the priests, were thirteen cities with their suburbs (Joshua 21:19).**

- Judah and Simeon combined releases nine cities (out of the 13 chosen) for the Kohathite-priests: Joshua 21:9-16

- Benjamin takes up the sum total of the remaining 4 cities: Joshua 21:17-18

The power of genealogy and generational notation connects strongly with recognition of a prophet's origin. For example, Jeremiah (Compare Joshua 21:17-18 with Jeremiah 1:1) is from the Kohathite family line in Benjamin. It is very logical Jeremiah would not only become a priest but a prophetic priest because of his ancestral connection to Kohath being placed in Benjamin. Again, Jeremiah is a Benjaminite, Levitical-Priest and Prophet from the Kohath ancestral line. And it is in the same territory of

Benjamin that the Levitical Prophetic Capitals of Gibeah and Ramah are born (1 Samuel 10:5-7; 1 Samuel 19:18-24).

The remaining ten cities distributed to the other Kohathite families among Ephraim, Manasseh and Dan are equally important. Their presence provides clarity to the other remaining prophetic capitals in scripture:

***All the cities were ten with their suburbs for the families of the children of Kohath that remained (Joshua 21:26)***

- **Ephraim releases four cities to the remaining non-priestly Kohathites: Joshua 21:20-22**
- **Dan releases four cities: Joshua 21:23-24**
- **The ½ Tribe of Manasseh releases the sum total of two cities: Joshua 21:25**

It is highly likely that the remaining prophetic schools of Jericho, Gilgal and Bethel were very close in proximity. Joshua's traveling into the land of Canaan revealed Gilgal and Jericho's close proximity:

***And the people came up out of Jordan on the tenth day of the first month, and encamped in Gilgal, in the eat border of Jericho (Joshua 4:19).***

The key indicator of the Jordan still being present during the days of Elijah's school of prophets among Bethel and Jericho confirmed this was the same place Joshua encamped when entering Israel (2 Kings 2:4-5, 7-8, 13). Jericho was explained to be not far from the Jordan. And according to Joshua 4:19, Gilgal and Jericho are neighbors with Gilgal being east of Jericho. So Bethel is not that far from Jericho.

This is how Elijah can travel the same day to both Bethel and Jericho before his transition. These three neighboring cities are within similar families of territories. That particular territory belonged to Benjamin and were closely connected to Joseph's sons (Ephraim and Manasseh's territory):

*"...This was the inheritance of the children of Benjamin, by the coasts thereof round about, according to their families. Now the cities of the tribe of the children of Benjamin according to their families were Jericho...and Bethel...and Ramah...Gibeath (Joshua 18:20b-21a, 22b, 25b, 28b).*

*And the lot of the children of Joseph fell from Jordan by Jericho, unto the water of Jericho on the east, to the wilderness that goeth up from Jericho throughout mount Bethel...So the children of Joseph, Manasseh and Ephraim, took their inheritance (Joshua 16:1, 4).*

Jericho, Bethel, Gibeah and Ramah are in or near the territory of Benjamin. These are four prophetic cities out of the five. And Gilgal is not that far from Gibeah because Samuel instructs Saul to go to down to Gilgal and wait to sacrifice there with him:

*And thou shalt go down before me to Gilgal; and, behold I will come down unto thee, to offer burnt offerings, and to sacrifice sacrifices of peace offerings, seven days shalt thou tarry, till I come to thee, and shew thee what thou shalt do (1 Samuel 10:8).*

Again, the Kohathite families received four cities from Ephraim and two from half of Manasseh. It is highly probable that Elijah and Elisha's sons of prophets' paradigm are all descendants of Kohathite family origins. Their diaspora can be connected either to Ephraim or Manasseh, but it's strongly possible that they are from Benjamin. The evolution of the prophetic family and ministry covers the entire nation. This still confirms any prophet's origin back to the foundational association of the Kohathite bloodline.

For example: Anna, who is of the tribe of Asher can closely be connected to Ephraim and Manasseh: Joshua 17:10. It is possible that her descendants mingled with Kohathite descendants, thus creating her prophetic presence purpose during the temple encounter with Jesus Christ: (Luke 2:36).

We must wholly conclude if there was not a Levitical diaspora, then there would have never become the need for the relevance of prophetic capitals. One is the offspring of the other. If Simeon and Levi had not done what they did, in retaliation for Dinah, and if the firstborn of Egypt were not taken by the death angel, then possibly Levi and his descendants would have not been the tribe chosen to fulfill this task.

The assignment would have probably fallen upon Reuben's children, but Levi was apparently predestined by the foreknowledge of God to become God's tithe from his people. And there is greater implication of the ownership of God's prophets within this same regard. Prophets are also a tithe unto God. They are God's representatives and mouthpiece. In fact, the purpose of the Levitical diaspora aids and assists Israel with the benefit of staying connected to the presence of God by way of their Levitical association.

So there is clear relevance for the presence of Levitical diaspora and capitals. Because a diaspora creates a capital and therefore the Levitical diaspora birth the prophetic capitals of Old Testament scripture. When the capitals were first created, they were produced with = high purity. Within the latter days, the prophetic family, diaspora and capitals became polluted (Ezekiel Chapter 8). This is the case even today. The oil was purified as Malachi predicted, and with this new purity, the new prophetic family, Diaspora and Capitals is sure to follow.

We who are prophetic must accept that we are adopted, engrafted or legally born into a prophetic family. If one is not literally of a Jewish descent than their prophetic mantle is grandfathered into the prophetic family of God by way of the blood of our Lord Jesus Christ. He is the current generation that all prophets can be directly associated with, and his generation connects back to even the original prophetic generation of Levi. So it's very important that today's prophets are not prophetic nomads. It's equally important to locate your prophetic home or capital. Therein within that capital lies the correct generation and generational leader.

The last importance is the understanding of the relational value of being prophetically released in your correct region and environment. Thus, your prophetic career is intricately connected to your proper alignment to the proper prophetic capital that shows your prophetic family's lineage. You should become interested in learning not only the prophetic history of your generation, but the migration of your leader. Learning the evolution of their prophetic history, intricately wrapped in their vision will allow you to have clear vision of your very own prophetic assignment.

This is not a haphazard experience. And one that is not an overnight and straightway property. But the location of such truths is only accomplished through much prayer and fasting. Not forgetting heavy discernment, even with a thoroughly submitted heart, these contributing actions will play vital roles in your deliverance of prophetic displacement. Levi's generation starts with the same common purpose: Worship. Worship service and service positions then grew to other realities. We cannot just start with the prophetic and be successful. We have to start with the origin of what type of prophetic purpose our generation's assignment expresses. Then we can matriculate to individual purposes.

The season of the individual prophecy is over! The Bible says "every word is established in the mouth of two or three witnesses." There is no private interpretation of prophesying and being prophetic (2 Peter 1:10). Therefore, every prophet should be accountable to someone and somewhere. Every prophet needs a home, a starting point and traceable diaspora connecting them to a specific prophetic network and family of God. Therein reveals the relevance of this intricate study of diaspora and capitals.

# 5

# Nomad or Civilized?

## THE CONNECTION OF OLD & NEW PROPHETIC-CAPITALS

### A Review of the Original Prophetic Capitals

Instead of just seeing them as mere cities, we now must view them as **the first prophetic capitals of scripture**. And before they were prophetic capitals, these locations were known historical sites of Israelite history. The order mentioned below is solely based on their order of prophetic occurrence and not historical origin. The Old Testament records five known prophetic communities (that we will call prophetic capitals):

- **Gibeah**
- **Ramah**
- **Bethel**
- **Gilgal**
- **Jericho**

**Gibeah** is the hometown of the first king of Israel – Saul (1 Samuel 10:26). **Ramah** is the hometown of the last judge of Israel and Prophet, Samuel (1 Samuel 25:1). **Bethel** is made famous by Jacob, who dreams about a ladder filled with angels descending and ascending unto God (Genesis 28:10-19). **Gilgal** is the starting point where Joshua leads the children of Israel into the Promised Land (Joshua 4:19-20). And **Jericho** is the infamous place Israel marched around a grand total of thirteen times and then shouts until its walls disintegrate (Joshua 6:20). God later instructs the people never to rebuild Jericho, saying any man who lays foundation would curse themselves and future generations. Each of these cities scripturally is recorded as portions of Benjamin's territory:

***Now the cities of the tribe of Benjamin according to their families were Jericho...and Bethel...and Ramah...And Zelah, Eleph, and Jebusi, which is Jerusalem, Gibeath, and Kirjath: fourteen cities with their villages. This is the inheritance of the children of Benjamin according to their families (Joshua 18:21a, 22b, 25a, 28).***

And within these five famous places of mere civilian life came an even greater purpose. That purpose is prophetic life! They became cities of Levitical and prophetic presence, and the evolution of the Levitical diaspora causes the drastic shift of these cities, making them prophetic capitals. The five cities are also clustered into two groupings by their historical and prophetic connections:

- **Group #1: Gibeah & Ramah –**
  **(The Band of Prophets' Era)**

- **Group #2: Bethel; Gilgal; Jericho –**
  **(The Sons of Prophets Era)**

There is a 400-year interval between the two prophetic family clusters mentioned. Just as there is a 400-year interval between the prophetic generation of Moses, Miriam and Aaron. Within these next two prophetic generations we have our second and third witnesses for the importance of the presence of a prophetic generation and prophetic family:

- Moses, Miriam and Aaron are our first witnesses to this truth.

- The Bands of Prophets Era is our second witnesses to this truth.

- The Sons of Prophets Era is our third witnesses to this truth.

We must also realize these prophetic capitals still possess a habitation of regular citizens who I term *non-prophetic citizens* per each prophetic capital. As a result of the prophetic presence within the corresponding city, each city becomes prophetically conducive to the anointing of the residing prophetic family and their prophetic leader. If you extract Kohath's life from each of these given environments, no city would possess the title of being a prophetic capital. <u>For prophetic capitals only remain prophetic if prophetic people remain residents.</u>

The greater the prophetic presence within a given city determines the measurement of prophetic power for that city. And each of the first two cities equally possesses a major influence of prophetic power within them. Those cities are none other than the neighboring cities of Ramah and Gibeah.

## The Band of Prophets Paradigm (Gibeah and Ramah)

The days of the prophetic capitals of Gibeah and Ramah were called the "company" or "band of prophets" era. Both Ramah and Gibeah are filled with heavy Benjaminite and Kohathite presences. The Benjamite presence are the non-prophetic citizens. And the Kohathite presence are the prophetic-citizens. Within this era, Samuel created systematic structures of Levitical praise and worship teams which become the first fruits of tabernacle and temple prophetic music ministry.

The band of prophets are not blatantly clarified as being Levitical anywhere within the texts used, but when they are mentioned, you can see residue of Levitical properties upon the musical prophets of Gibeah (1 Samuel 10:5-7). Further research within other scripture reveals how Samuel's connection to the band of prophets is of a Levitical nature. In fact, Samuel is from the family line of Kohath. His father's descendants are from Kohath's second born son, Izhar:

| The descendants of Kohath: |
|---|
| Amminadab his son, Korah his son, |
| Assir his son, Elkanah his son, |
| Ebiasaph his son, Assir his son, |
| Tahath his son, Uriel his son, |
| Uzziah his son, and Shaul his son |
| **The descendants of Elkanah:** |
| Amasai, Ahimoth, |
| Elkanah his son, Zophai his son, |
| Nahath his son, Eliab his son, |
| Jeroham his son, Elkanah his son and Samuel his son |
| **The sons of Samuel:** |
| Joel the firstborn |

> And Abijah the second son (1 Chronicles 6:22-28, NIV)

The labor necessary while reviewing genealogies often causes people to ignore the major point and purpose of its presence within scripture. Again, genealogy shows lineage, and lineage explains history. History opens portals to revelation. The longer one studies a genealogy, the greater revelations can illuminate. For example, the revelation of Samuel's connection to Levi is seen in this referenced genealogy above. From the union of Elkanah and Hannah, Samuel is born (1 Samuel 1:19-20). However, Samuel is given back to God in response to God's blessing of Hannah's womb (1 Samuel 1:11 and Numbers 3:12). Hannah and Elkanah would have three more sons and two daughters after Samuel:

***"And the Lord visited Hannah, so that she conceived, and bare three sons and two daughters..." (1 Samuel 2:21a)***

Technically, Hannah and Elkanah had four sons, including Samuel. All six children are of the Kohathite bloodline (1 Samuel 1:5b). Not to mention, Peninnah, Elkanah's second wife, has an undisclosed large amount of children from their union (1 Samuel 1:2). How they are mentioned within this list is not clear. Is it by each wife? Or is it by just a single bloodline? Whatever the strategy, God clearly reveals Samuel's connection to Levi. He shows that Kohath is the origination. Korah is another descendent and Elkanah, his father, is connected.

When isolating this text alone it can be very confusing. But going further into the next verses, hinting breadcrumbs lead us further to the connection of Samuel's blood relation to that of

Levitical and Kohathite origins. Samuel's bloodline is the same as Moses, Miriam and Aaron:

**<u>These and their sons served of the Kohathites: Heman</u>, the singer, the son of Joel, <u>the son of Samuel</u>** *[the great prophet and judge].* **The son of Elkanah [III], the son of Jeroham, the son of Eliel, the son of Toah, the son of Zuph, the son of Elkanah [II], the son of Mahath, the son of Amasai, the son of Elkanah [i], the son of Joel, the son of Azariah, the son of Zephaniah, the son of Tahath, the son of Assir, the son of Ebiasaph, the son of Korah, the son of Izhar, the son of Kohath, the son of Levi, the son of Israel (Jacob). (1 Chronicles 6:33-38, Amplified Version).**

When David sets up the first worship in the Tabernacle/Temple Era, he uses Samuel's firstborn grandson, Heman to lead the singing. If you start with verse 38 and read backwards to verse 33, you can see how Israel (Jacob) leads you to Heman, by way of Kohath and Izhar, who are all of the Levitical family:

- Verse 38: Israel to Levi; Levi to Kohath; Kohath to Izhar (Kohath's second born)

- Verse 37: Reveals Korah is a child of Izhar, who is a son of Kohath

- Verse 34a & 33b: Reveals Heman's family line is of Samuel, making Heman Samuel's grandson

When reading the first verse of 1 Samuel 1:1, we can misunderstand the citizenship of Elkanah if we have not learned the truth behind Levitical Diasporas. Even though Elkanah is mentioned as being a citizen of Ramathaim-Zophim, an **Ephrathite** (1 Samuel 1:1), he is also a Kohathite. Elkanah's family and forefathers are placed in Ephraim's territory (see Chapter 4). Elkanah's family is of the Kohathite clan. Elkanah and his wives were of Mt. Ephraim, but at the time of this storyline they actually lived in Ramah. This now clarifies how Samuel is a Kohathite citizen of Ramah instead of Ephraim like his father's family:

**And Elkanah went to Ramah to his house. And the child did minister unto the Lord before Eli the priest (1 Samuel 1:11)**

This was also said of Naomi's husband and sons:

**"...And a certain man of Bethelehem-Judah went to sojourn in the country of Moab, he, and his wife, and his two sons. And the name of the man was Elimelech, and the name of his wife Naomi, and the name of his two sons Mahlon and Chilion, Ephrathites of Bethlehem-Judah..." (Ruth 1:1b-2a, KJV).**

The Levitical people did move from town to town. Even if their ancestry was originally assigned to a specific place their assignment of being Levitical would prompt them to move. And here is another example of a Levite being declared a citizen of particular city, even though their Levitical lineage starts within another city:

**And there was a young man out of Bethlehem-Judah of the family of Judah, who was a Levite, and he sojourned there. And the man departed out of the city from Bethlehem-Judah to sojourn where he could find a place: and he came to mount Ephraim to the house of Micah, as he journeyed. And Micah said unto him, whence comest thou? And he said**

*unto him, I am a Levite of Bethlehem-Judah, and I go to sojourn where I may find a place. And Micah said unto him, dwell with me, and be unto me a father and a priest, and I will give thee ten shekels of silver by the year, and a suit of apparel, and thy victuals, so the Levite went in. And the Levite was content to dwell with the man; and the young man was unto him as one of his sons. And Micah consecrated the Levite: and the young man because his priest, and was in the house of Micah. Then said Micah, now know I that the Lord will do me good, seeing I have a Levite to my priest (Judges 17:7-13).*

Samuel's family's citizenship may have been of Joseph's son, Ephraim's territory. But their true citizenship was the Kohathite and musical family of Izhar. This further explains the possible reasoning behind the production of the first musical and prophetic guild of musicians coming down from the hillside of Gibeah (1 Samuel 10:5-7).

There was a strong prophetic anointing in both Gibeah and Ramah. These cities were heavily populated with the presence of the prophetic and the Kohathite Levitical family. Ramah's confirmation is also seen when David is fleeing from Saul who sent a series of messengers to Ramah for the apprehension of David. When they arrived, they experienced the power of prophecy apprehending them:

*So David fled, and escaped, and came to Samuel to Ramah, and told him all that Saul had done to him. And he and Samuel went and dwelt in Naioth. And it was told Saul, saying, behold, David is at Naioth in Ramah. And Saul sent messengers to take David: and when they saw <u>the company</u>*

***of prophets prophesying, and Samuel standing as appointed over them**, the Spirit of God was upon the messengers of Saul, and they also prophesied. And when it was told Saul, he sent other messengers, and they prophesied likewise, and Saul sent messengers again the third time, and they prophesied also. Then went he also to Ramah, and came to a great well that is in Sechu: and he asked and said, where are Samuel and David? And one said, behold, they be at Naioth in Ramah. And he went thither to Naioth in Ramah: and the Spirit of God was upon him also, and he went on, and prophesied until he came to Naioth in Ramah. And he stripped off his clothes also, and prophesied before Samuel in like manner, and lay down naked all that day and all that night. (1 Samuel 19:19-23a).*

The influential presence of the company of prophets within Ramah is similar to the functioning of the band of prophets at Gibeah (1 Samuel 10:5-7). But in Samuel's hometown of Ramah, we see Samuel literally standing among this particular company of prophets. He led them in the practicing of the prophetic anointing, and the anointing of the prophets and Ramah was so rich that anyone coming into their prophetic presence would automatically shift into a prophetic tangent.

Kohath had 8,600 people to divide among four and half territories. That's a lot of prophetic presence in each town, and these are the only two instances recorded in scripture of a place being so prophetically influential. The secondary reasoning that the prophetic power is very similar in both towns is because one cannot deny Samuel's association with both cities. This is why Ramah and Gibeah can be termed prophetic sisters and capitals. In fact, they are mere prophetic twins.

Yes, these two cites shows the influential power of prophecy. Gibeah and Ramah further explained the importance of cooperative teamwork within a prophetic community and family. The twin cities demonstrate the potential of prophetic influence. The power of prophecy can change a given society. I strongly believe a clarion call and a prophetic cry for the manifestation of New Gibeahs and Ramahs are in order.

Ramah and Gibeah flowed under a Levitical, musical, priestly, and prophetic assignment. Their master prophet, Samuel, taught the importance of worship and upholding prophetic positioning. This revealed that the responsibility of the prophet is the assistance of a people finding God. Therefore, these prophetic and Levitical generations, within both towns, possess similar assignments that now reverberate within our spirits.

## The Sons of the Prophets Paradigm
## (Gilgal, Bethel and Jericho)

Four hundred years later, between 900-800 B.C), God established another prophetic guild. This era of prophetic presence comes with successive leadership. The first leader of the prophetic community and capital was the famous prophet, Elijah. And his prophetic successor was the equally famous prophet, Elisha. The location of their prophetic capitals were the cities Jericho, Bethel and Gilgal. And the days of their prophetic administration within those capitals were called the "sons of prophets" era.

When the transition of prophetic leadership occurred, Elijah traveled to each of his three prophetic capitals. It is believed that Gilgal was also visited because the territory is the first mentioned. 2 Kings 2:1; 2 and Kings 4:38 confirms Gilgal as a prophetic capital. Elijah visited all three of his prophetic groups before official transition of power was given. He first went to Gilgal (2 Kings 2:1), then Bethel (2 Kings 2:2), and finally Jericho (2 Kings 2:4).

The Sons of Prophets era drastically differs from the band of prophets' era which supported the legitimacy of genetic connection among prophetic sons. However, the Sons of Prophets era ironically held a heavier standard to its name. The period of the Sons of Prophets was not one that perpetuated the sole continuation of genetic connection.

However, it adds this dynamic. The process of spiritual adoption and spiritual fathering is first seen between Elijah and Elisha. This wasn't Elijah's choice, but it was God's. And just as a natural father cannot pick the creation and birth of his son, neither can a spiritual father do the same with whom God chooses:

**And the Lord said unto him, God, return on the way to the wilderness of Damascus: and when thou comest, anoint Hazel to be king over Syria: and Jehu the son of Nimshi shalt thou anoint to be king over Israel: <u>and Elisha the son of Shaphat of Abel-Meholah shalt thou anoint to be prophet in thy room</u>. (1 Kings 19:15-16).**

When referring to the sons of prophets, it is not clear if majority of prophets in each community were of natural descent. But it is quite clear that there are prophetic families within these guilds because the sons of prophets were allowed to marry:

**"Now there cried a certain woman of the wives of the sons of the prophets unto Elisha..." (2 Kings 4:1a)**

It's no longer about natural pedigree as much as it is about supernatural purpose. Just as the presence of Gibeah and Ramah taught the power of influence among the united efforts of a prophetic community, Gilgal, Jericho and Bethel had their major lesson. And that lesson was the power of a prophetic network.

When there is power within a network, there will be a union of prophetic demonstration. Individuality will never dissolve, but connection and clarity concerning events will not be of private interpretation. The sons of these three schools were equally connected to their prophetic leader, by way of the Spirit. They all received the same training; Elijah had taught them well. The influential and insightful lessons of both groups further demonstrate why we need the return of each unique and current prophetic generation.

The primary purpose of exclusively recording the five cities is to testify to the communal voice of the prophets. And they are created for the official recognition of a prophetic society among Israel. Other known events taken place within these cities are considered isolated events, but those turn of events usually have nothing to do with the credibility of the prophetic flow within that site—even if that site was a notorious site, creating heinous crimes or unfortunate circumstances such as incidents, prior at Jericho (Joshua 6; 1 Kings 16:34) and Gibeah (Judges 19).

## Prophetic Activity in Judah (David)

Historically, there is heavy prophetic activity in Judah. When David became king of Israel, he also contributed further to the organization of using legitimate prophetic families. The assignment is further seen in the temple and palace duties. It makes sense that David could use the prophetic in the nation's capital. For the tribe of Kohath was already preplaced there by Joshua:

**"Moreover David and the captains of the host separated to the service of the sons of Asaph, and of Heman, and of Jeduthun, who should prophesy wit harps, with psalteries and with cymbals: and the number of the workmen according to their service was..."(1 Chronicles 25:1)**

King David mimicked Samuel's prophetic paradigm and replicated a Levitical establishment. This paradigm started with Moses. Moses' paradigm was adopted by Samuel and later instituted by David. David was used prophetically and musically, even though he was not of the tribe of Levi.

Samuel's prophetic influence within the life of David was the necessary connection of Levi to David. After all, David was another template of the image of Jesus Christ being prophet, priest and king. This is why Judah became a primary capital for the perpetuation of the extensive Levitical diaspora. David was instrumental in making his own prophetic environment because he too understood the power of prophecy and how its influence and insight helps a nation.

For example, five of Israel's sons (Dan, Simeon, Judah, Benjamin, Joseph) house the four sons belonging to the descendants of Kohath. These five territories given to Kohath's children within Canaan become the first fruits and initial trademark explaining the greater truth behind the necessity of having modern day prophetic communities.

Judah, Benjamin, and, on some occasions, Ephraim became the strongest lands for the prophetic anointing and family. Even as the prophetic voice takes its siesta (after the ministry of Malachi until the time of Zecharias and his son John), the prophetic never lost its purpose of connection and community. It simply waited for the next era in which it found reason to flourish and manifest. After Jesus' earthly ministry the administration of the apostles take the scene, and the prophetic once again begins to emerge. Instead of just establishing Jewish lands, its new manifestation reaches beyond Israel and goes into the cities of Greece and Asia.

## Modern Day Examples of Prophetic Diasporas: Antioch & Ephesus

*James, a servant of God and of the Lord Jesus Christ, to the twelve tribes which are scattered abroad, greeting. (James 1:1)*

The bishop of Jerusalem, James, speaks about how the original tribes were still dispersed. As he addresses them in his letter, we get the sense that it's bigger than Levi; Israel has experienced a universal diaspora. And this metaphor can be taken literally. Intense persecution of all Jewish-Christians in Jerusalem caused a massive exodus into the tri-fold regions of Galilee, Samaria and Jerusalem:

*"And they were all scattered throughout the regions of Judea and Samaria, except the apostles" (Acts 8:1b)*

Eventually the persecution caused another diaspora of Jewish-Christians from the trifold regions of Jerusalem, Samaria and Galilee into the uttermost parts of the world. The population of Christians became a mix multitude. The population expanded to Jew and Greek alike, and conversion reached the regions of Antioch:

*Now they which were scattered abroad upon the persecution that arose about Stephan traveled as far as Phenice, and Cyprus, and Antioch, preaching the word to none but unto the Jews only. And some of them were men of Cyprus and Cyrene, which, when they were come to*

***Antioch, spake unto the Grecians, preaching the Lord Jesus (Acts 11:19-20).***

Antioch was a Grecian city filled with Jewish presence. As a result of this church growth, a new prophetic community emerged. But their presence was not clarified until Paul's ministry: Paul was in Antioch for a year where he was in the presence of a presbytery of prophets. These prophets were possibly a mixture of once Jewish and Greek prophets who had become Christian. These same prophets released Paul and Barnabas into the first missionary journey into the Asia Minor. His duration in Antioch was one that showcased this experience of when there was more than one prophet in a church.

**"Now there were in the church that was at Antioch certain prophets..." (Acts 13:1a)**

When Paul later traveled to Ephesus in Asia, he stayed for three years. While there, ministered to 12 disciples of John. After their conversion, they experienced the gifts of tongues and prophecy:

***"...Paul having passed through the upper coasts came to Ephesus: and finding certain disciples...And when Paul had laid his hands upon them, the Holy Ghost came on them; and they spake with tongues, and prophesied. And all the men were about twelve" (Acts 19:1b, 6-7)***

Antioch and Ephesus can serve as supernatural territories allotted to release the return of a communal-prophetic anointing. Both are the results of a blend of Jewish and Christian diaspora which was created from a spirit of persecution. Within every affliction, there is greater purpose.

And regardless of the factors surrounding Antioch and Ephesus, both show strong prophetic presence as potentials for deputizing them as New Testament prophetic capitals. The next place is the greatest example.

*Apostle Sherman D. Farmer*

## The Greatest Modern Day Example of a Prophetic Capital: Corinth

*For God is not the author of confusion, but of peace, as in all churches of the saints....Let all things be done decently and in order (1 Corinthians 14:33, 40, KJV).*

Within the dual testimony of Antioch and Ephesus, another witness came forth. The third witness was the city of Corinth which is our chief example of the New Testament's example of reproducing a prophetic capital. Corinth is scripturally known for its prophetic climate as discussed within Paul's writings (1 Corinthians Chapters 11 – 14).

Corinth has the largest known amount of prophets within its congregation (next to Antioch). Paul resided in Corinth for almost two years. Within the two years, spiritual gifts and offices manifested. Thus, Corinth becomes our chief example of a modern day prophetic capital within New Testament scripture.

I didn't immediately realize how Corinth paralleled and personified our present example of the former Old Testament prophetic capitals. Corinth has a large number of prophets like Antioch (Acts 13:1). Both Antioch and Corinth surely can be likened unto the ancient sites of Gibeah and Ramah. While the prophetic presence within Ephesus, Rome and Thessalonica can be the resemblance of the prophetic schools of Gilgal, Bethel and Jericho.

His first letter to the church of Corinth is actually our divine blueprint for prophetic government among prophetic families. It helps govern the presence of the prophetic people. And after many years of pondering with intense observation, I now draw this likely conclusion. There is clear reasoning why Paul was adamant about the clarity and coveting of the gift of prophecy. Paul charges men to understand all the words declared apostolically from his mouth and through his pen were in fact God's commandments directly dispensed through Him and from the Holy Spirit. Even when organizing the prophetic order and flow within the house of the Corinthian churches, he stated this bold resolve:

**If any man think himself to be a prophet, or spiritual, let him acknowledge that the things that I write unto you are the commandments of the Lord (1 Corinthians 14:37).**

From another point of view, Corinth's prophetic organization could have been formatted because of Paul's training. Benjamin was a territory filled with heavy prophetic and Levitical inclinations. These inclinations were among all of its towns and therefore its citizens. And the Bible clearly reveals Paul's tribal heritage is of Benjamin. This strongly implies that Paul could have been of a Kohathite, priestly and Levitical ancestry, placing him within the propensity of receiving the true connection to prophetic origin:

**Circumcised the eighth day, of the stock of Israel, of the tribe of Benjamin, a Hebrew of Hebrews; as touching the law, a Pharisee (Philippians 3:5, KJV)**

***"...For I also am an Israelite, of the seed of Abraham, of the tribe of Benjamin." (Romans 11:1b, KJV)***

Not to mention Paul's heavy training as a Pharisee. He possessed a vast knowledge about the Old Testament. And this contributing factor could have been the source of inspiration that created these models. The reproduction of the timeless principles Paul used in Corinth are like the master prophets of the Old Testament (i.e. Moses, Samuel, Elijah and Elisha).

The church of Corinth sustained heavy demonic attacks, and the presence and subject of prophecy was surely one of those satanic tactics of opposition. When dealing with the prophetic problems of this Greek town, it is quite possible Paul used some of those same values as a means of rebuking and casting out the spirits of error and confusion. This paradigm of information is necessary for application when a pastor is dealing with a large number of prophetic congregants. Paul's further clarity to the church of Corinth should help all who pastors prophetically and/or pastors prophetic people.

## Conclusion

Prophetic diaspora is still applicable. Even if they are not of a Kohathite or Levitical context, the purposes of such entities are still the same. Regardless if we call the prophetic places Gibeah, Ramah, Jericho, Gilgal, Bethel, Corinth, Ephesus, or Antioch we have enough scriptural witness from both Testaments which demonstrates this reality is necessary.

**Old Testament Capitals:**

- Gibeah
- Ramah
- Jericho
- Bethel
- Gilgal

**New Testament Capitals:**

- Antioch
- Corinth
- Ephesus
- Thessalonica
- Rome

So there must be a prophetic place for a prophetic people. Just as Eden was for Adam and Eve, these cities were for the prophets of the Old and New Testaments. Where is your Gibeah, Ramah, Gilgal, Jericho, Bethel, Antioch, Corinth, or Ephesus? For within reside your generational purpose, relevance and growth.

It's about building a prophetic community with accountability. You are not your own. You belong to God and a people like Levi and his sons, Moses and his siblings, Samuel and his band of prophets, and Elijah and Elisha with the sons of prophets. We must belong somewhere accountable to our prophetic father's leadership.

If one is truly seeking the prophetic purposes of God, then you will aggressively engage to find the family of prophets which matches your DNA and unique call. The options are nomad prophet or civilized prophet. Which one are you?

# 6

# *Son or Bastard?*

## THE REEMERGENCE OF TRUE PROPHETIC FATHERS & SONS

### The Incidents of Gibeah and Ramah

*And it came to pass, when all that knew him beforetime saw that, behold, he prophesied among the prophets, then the people said one to another, What is this that is come unto the son of Kish? Is Saul also among the prophets? And one of the same place answered and said, <u>but who is their father</u>? Therefore it became a proverb, is Saul also among the prophets? (1 Samuel 10:11-12, KJV)*

*"...Wherefore they say, Is Saul also among the prophets" (1 Samuel 19:24b)*

The non-prophetic citizens of Ramah and Gibeah had a great reaction. When they witnessed Saul prophesying among the company of prophets in both towns, their thoughts became unanimous with this behavior. The tone in the text suggests one of surprise, slight disgust and also of grave concern. They seemed offended and very shocked, watching Saul with high scrutiny.

It didn't make any sense to them. Bear in mind that these communities were well-knit populations, and everyone knew of his own generation. Apparently working knowledge of all generations within the community was known and accepted. So their blatant asking if Saul was one "now one of the prophets" shows disapproval of Saul's new assertion within the prophetic work. To them, he was not a prophet. He was a man's son of the tribe of Benjamin. And his actions and activity among the prophets was unacceptable.

Another asked, *"Where is their father?"* This question shows the importance of prophetic accountability which takes shape within an organized and legitimate prophetic community. Many people in the church wonder this very same thing when they hear of a new prophet's emergence. Who birthed you? And who is your covering? These are rightful questions and should have a ready answer!

Even the Prophet's Amos' hang-ups about prophesying reveal this same confirmation:

**Then answered Amos, and said to Amaziah, I was no prophet, neither was I a prophet's son; but I was a herdman, and a gatherer of sycamore fruit (Amos 7:14).**

When God called Amos, he responded with his realization of no direct connection to any prophetic family, father or prophetic community. Incidents at Gibeah and Ramah further supports the necessity of the reemergence of prophetic families, principles, protocols, and orders. Within that paradigm, there is high importance. And the highest importance is the return of the prophetic father and son paradigm.

The non-prophetic people of Gibeah and Ramah understood that there were protocols, principles and paradigms. The prophetic guild and calling is the protective mechanism necessary to stop bastard examples of illegitimate prophetic demonstrations. The towns of Gibeah and Ramah knew it was primary directive for you to have lineage and clear affiliation. A prophet must have an authentic relationship to a legitimate organization. And when the people saw Saul, there was a great uproar! The question again arises: Who is your prophetic father?

Prophetic parenting is still needed within the body of Christ. Prophetic children still need the socialization of other prophetic people. The prophetic community is the means of providing prophetic sobriety and sanctification within their prospective callings. As quoted in Proverbs 27:17, iron sharpens iron. And as written in 1 Corinthians 14:32, the spirit of the prophet is subject to the prophet.

Therefore, each level of ecclesiastical office has its own community whereby it is sharpened and held accountable. And its community is sharpened and governed by logical pecking order of those who have been measured by their grace, position, purpose and distinct mantle. Simply put, some are called to father and some are called to serve as sons. This principle is the same principle we found in the Garden of Eden with Adam and his sons. Therefore, a prophetic community is the true resolution for the dissolution of current prophetic abominations. And these random prophetic hybrids that are illegally emerging must be purified, and in some cases, evicted from their self-assumed position. After all, combating the manifestation of false prophets is also a responsibility of the true prophet.

When it came to the protocols of Gibeah and Ramah, you were literally born through a natural pedigree of a legitimate prophetic family. You couldn't just arbitrarily assume the calling without corporate validation of a given prophetic association. And again, this is why the non-prophetic citizens of Gibeah and Ramah were certainly startled at the connection of Saul to the prophetic during his two moments in Gibeah and Ramah. In context, it was not Saul's intention to assume a prophetic mantle or calling. The initial prophetic experience was to motivate him for his new assignment as king; the second experience was a means of diversion from further physical harming of David:

**And when all who knew Saul before saw that he spoke by inspiration among the [schooled] prophets, the people said one to another, what has come over [him, who is nobody but] the son of Kish? Is Saul also among the prophets? One from that same place answered, but who is the father of the others? So it became a proverb, is Saul also among the prophets? (Amplified Version)**

Israel only felt comfortable when there was the presence of a prophetic father. When there were many prophets stationed in one place, the people felt safe. For Gibeah and Ramah, Samuel was their designated leader. And this further teaches how the paradigm of the prophetic family, along with its protocols and principles, certainly helps keep order among the presence of an accumulative number of prophets. But the importance of this reference is to also notice how they declared and viewed the presence of the prophetic community! They viewed it as the same organism God gave Adam and Eve to create. That organism is called a family:

**Wherefore they say, Is Saul among the prophets? (1 Samuel 19:23b, KJV) – The Response of the Non-Prophetic Citizens of Ramah.**

<u>**But who is the father of the others? (1 Samuel 10:12b – Amp)**</u>

"Is he a son of the prophets now?" and "I thought he was a Benjamite!" and "I thought he was a son of Kish (which implies not of Levi and therefore not a true prophet)." Their questioning teaches that protocols, principles and family-oriented paradigms for the prophetic anointing were visible and well-respected throughout that current period of Israelite history.

Your connection to a prophetic leader was just as important during the times of the Old Testament as it is now within the last days of the New Testament Era. The revelation is clear. We need to see prophetic parents as well as prophetic children. There needs to be a full presentation of unity and compliance. This is the only way the church can healthily receive anyone's asserted prophetic mantle. When this becomes a consistent practice, the purity of prophecy will begin again.

And we surely need to see the prophetic families used generationally, not just individually or under the bastardly flow as a rogue or renegade. This strongly confirms and supports this revelation. God requires relationship and fellowship among the prophetic family. When there is proper functioning of a prophetic family, this brings true ease among non-prophetic people's and other Christian-oriented communities.

***But this is that which was spoken by the prophet Joel; And it shall come to pass in the last days, Saith God, I will pour out my Spirit upon all flesh: and your sons and your daughters shall prophesy, and your young men shall see visions, and your old men shall dream dreams: And on my servants and on my handmaidens I will pour out in those days of my Spirit; and they shall prophesy (Acts 2:16-18).***

This is the season of the prophetic families' return. The sons and daughters are prophetically induced now. They are just waiting for prophetic fathers and mothers who are truly called by God to parent them. Samuel was a great father to the band and company of prophets' era. Moses was a great father to the prophetic siblings that helped him lead Israel from Egypt to the threshold of the Promised Land. But there is one more example of biblical clarity concerning prophetic fathering. Elijah is our final Old Testament witness of this truism.

*Apostle Sherman D. Farmer*

## The Incidents of Gilgal, Bethel & Jericho

*And it came to pass, when the Lord would take up Elijah into heaven by a whirlwind, that Elijah went with Elisha from Gilgal. And Elijah said unto Elisha, tarry here, I pray thee; for the Lord hath sent me to Bethel. And Elisha said unto him, as the Lord liveth, and as thy soul liveth, I will not leave thee. So they went down to Bethel. And the sons of the prophets that were at Bethel came forth to Elisha, and said unto him, knowest thou not that the Lord will take away thy master from thy head today? And he said, yea, I know it, hold ye your peace. (2 Kings 2:1-3).*

A major turning point happened 400 years between Samuel's Levitical and prophetic paradigm in comparison to Moses, Miriam and Aaron's paradigm. Four hundred years later, through Samuel, God created prophetic adoption into the program of the prophetic family. And that leadership of prophetic parenting is none other than the prophet Elijah. What's interesting to clarify is the obscurity of Elijah's tribal pedigree. Elijah's lineage and origin is not specified, but prior to his timely transition, in the beginning of Elijah's ministry, God instructed that Elisha would become his successor. And Elisha was not a natural descendent of Elijah, so he became the first adopted spiritual son. A prophetic son of no blood relation became the next prophetic father to the nation of prophets.

Elisha would also become the prophetic successor that would maintain Elijah's anointing within the earth. And Elisha is the next prophetic generational leader among the sons of prophets. The name Sons of Prophets is interesting because there is no further evidence supporting natural lineage. Elisha was a loyal prophetic son to his prophetic father. This is why he never leaves Elijah's side. Even through tour of duty and day, the course and shift of power came. Notice the text: Elijah went to each prophetic family. As he traveled, he noticed that Elisha went with him. He requested Elisha to stay at each place, but Elisha insisted on continuing with his leader:

*"....Tarry here, I pray thee: for the Lord hath sent me to Bethel..." (2 Kings 2:1b).*

*"...Tarry here, I pray thee: for the Lord hath sent me to Jericho..." (2 Kings 2:4b).*

Elisha knew his assignment. He would not stay. And he remained loyal and connected. What is amazing about the sons of prophetic community is their powerful connection. For the prophetic community all knew Elijah's time was come. All the children of Elijah knew, but it was for Elijah to remain directly with him:

*"And the Sons of the prophets that were at Bethel came forth unto Elisha...." (2 Kings 2:3a).*

*"And the Sons of the prophets that were at Jericho came to Elisha..." (2 Kings 2:5a).*

The same format isn't done when mentioning Gilgal, but it is certainly implied:

**And it came to pass, when the Lord would take up Elijah into heaven by a whirlwind, that Elijah went with Elisha from Gilgal (2 Kings 2:1).**

The protocol for the prophetic family anointing is very important when it comes to succession. The purpose of succession is just as important as the phenomenon of apostolic succession. The mantle of a leader is to stay in the earth because the Spirit of God has never left the earth. It is the person that leaves and not their anointing. It is the assignment of a true son to further carry the mantle of his father and to complete his own ministry.

The storyline of Elijah and Elisha shows the importance of prophetic inheritance. As Israel did with his sons, only can a prophetic father can do with his sons. This inheritance comes out of relationship, fellowship, obedience and faithfulness to a father's work. Jesus told Mary and Joseph that he was here to perform his father's business (Luke 2:49). It is the same with every prophetic son who should be about their prophetic father's work until God is ready to release them. A prophetic son will experience many difficulties without the presence of his prophetic father.

Elisha knew that he needed more than just the name of Master Prophet. He needed his prophetic father's anointing if he was going to lead. Elisha's posture teaches that a desire for a position as prophet never outweighs the actual assignment of being a prophet. Simply put, fruit is more important! For we are known by the fruit we bear. Not the titles we may carry. And this loyalty and unwavering commitment to his prophetic father is why Elisha received the anointing of becoming the next Master Prophet. Even today, there are many who want to be great prophets but don't understand that their release is intricately connected to their faithfulness. Faithfulness, loyalty and commitment are prerequisites for true impartation of prophetic inheritances (see also 2 Kings 3:11).

**And if ye have not been faithful in that which is another man's, who shall give you that which is your own? (Luke 16:12)**

Elisha knew he was destined to lead this large conglomerate of prophets. He was like a Prophetic Bishop once the mantle was ascertained. Elisha was destined to pastor the same three prophetic folds in three different regions formerly belonging to Elijah (2 Kings 2:7). This is why the prophetic sons of Elijah came together on that day. One, they came to see if they were the recipient of the prophetic blessing or inheritance from Elijah and his mantle. And two, they wanted to see who would receive the crown for the next leader.

The sons of the prophets all stood from afar, waiting to see the next shift of their prophetic leadership. Because Elisha was the faithful, consistent and the persistent one, he was foreordained by God to become the chosen son. This is why he was able to receive the prophetic blessing and impartation of fatherhood.

**And Elijah took his mantle, and wrapped it together, and smote the waters, and they were divided hither and thither, so that they two went over on dry ground. And it came to pass, when they were gone over, that Elijah said unto Elisha, ask what I shall do for thee, before I be taken away from thee. And Elisha said, I pray thee, let a double portion of thy spirit be upon me. And he said, thou hast asked a hard thing: nevertheless, if thou see me when I am taken from thee, it shall be so unto thee; but if no, it shall not be**

***so. And it came to pass, as they still went on, and talked, that, behold, there appeared a chariot of fire, and horses of fire, and parted them both asunder; and Elijah went up by a whirlwind into heaven. And Elisha saw it, and he cried, My father, my father, the chariot of Israel, and the horsemen thereof. And he saw him no more: and he took hold of his own clothes, and rent them in two pieces. (2 Kings 2:8-12).***

Notice crucial things that are taking place within this text. Elijah knew God informed him that Elisha was the chosen prophet in his room. So the connection between them was not unlikely. Neither was it displaced. Elisha's training in the prophetic had paid off, and his heart was clearly seen. When the separation from his prophetic father came, Elisha cried out. The cry for the loss of connection was more than for the succession of the prophetic anointing:

**"And Elisha saw it, and he cried, My father, my father..." (2 Kings 2:12a)**

He also had a clear vision of what was happening during the sight of the supernatural transport of the prophetic father. These are all indicators that Elisha's heart and abilities were seasoned and ready to be enhanced. The fusion of his anointing was ready to meet the power of his prophetic father's anointing. That combination is what makes a prophetic son prolific within his own ministry. Your anointing alone is not qualified. God has to impart and connect a son with his father so that proper identity may be assumed. And thus, a proper anointing will then be qualified to operate in the earth.

When the transition comes, the dissolving of former designations occur. No longer was Elijah the prophetic father; it was Elisha. No longer was Elisha considered a prophetic brother to his siblings; he automatically took on the role of the prophetic father. He had *big* shoes to fill. Elisha had many mouths to feed prophetically seeing that he had become the prophetic father unto all of Elisha's sons when the anointing transferred from Elijah.

**He took up also the mantle of Elijah that fell from him, and went back, and stood by the bank of Jordan: And he took the mantle of Elijah that fell from him, and smote the waters, and said, where is the lord God of Elijah? And when he also had smitten the waters, they parted hither and thither: and Elisha went over (2 Kings 2:13-14).**

Elisha had to first privately practice before he could publicly demonstrate the transfer of mantle. He knew that he couldn't get back to the previous level to assist the waiting sons until God manifested Himself through him, just as God had done with Elijah. Elisha performed the miracle of parting the waters of Jordan just as it was done by Elijah. This also teaches how well Elisha observed his spiritual father, as well as how prophetic discipleship is demonstrative and didactic. Discipleship isn't fruitful without fellowship. For Elisha had remained in fellowship and relationship well. And as a result of this then the mantle was fully passed. No longer would Elisha see himself as son, but he had to see himself as father.

**And when the sons of the prophets which were to view at Jericho saw him, they said, the Spirit of Elijah doth rest on**

***Elisha. And they came to meet him, and bowed themselves to the ground before him (2 Kings 2:15).***

Not only could he see himself as such, but so could the others. You cannot avoid your prophetic family lineage no more than you can avoid your spiritual father and leader. Every son should want to grow up and become a father; this is an innate desire of a man. So it is a supernatural desire for a spiritual child of a spiritual family.

Elisha was nothing without the leadership of Elijah. He would have never been able to become ready if his prophetic father did not teach him the ways of the prophet, including how to lead a prophetic people. Success was at his reach. Gilgal, Jericho and Bethel were all under the tutelage of Elisha, their new prophetic father. The prophetic generation is yet preserved because the spirit of Elijah now rests upon Elisha:

***And when the sons of the prophets which were to view at Jericho saw him, they said, The Spirit of Elijah doth rest on Elisha. And they came to meet him, and bowed themselves to the ground before him (2 Kings 3:15)***

For the father of such a ministry for the sons of prophets cannot start until the ministry of prophetic father begins. Elijah then Elisha became the father of many sons:

*"And a certain man of the sons of the prophets..." (1 Kings 20:35a)*

*"...the sons of Prophets that were at Bethel..." (2 Kings 2:3)*

*"...the sons of Prophet that were at Jericho..." (2 Kings 3:5)*

## The New Prophetic Generation

**And fifty men of the sons of the prophets went, and stood to view afar off: and they two stood by Jordan (2 Kings 3:7)**

But this simple process first started with Elisha's acceptance of who Elijah was to him. Certainly this is vice versa. Spiritual parenting is not to fill voids that natural parenting does not perform. Its primary function is to ensure the generational blessing and mantle is continued within a spiritual generation. Elisha had a natural father that he left on the day he met Elijah. However, the bond of his natural father was not greater than the bond of his spiritual father. His spiritual father was the father who was assigned to give him the importance of destiny.

**There came then his brethren and his mother, and, standing without, sent unto him, calling him. And the multitude sat about him, and they said unto him, Behold, thy mother and thy brethren without seek for thee. And he answered them, saying, Who is my mother, or my brethren? And he looked round about on them which say about him, and said, Behold my mother and my brethren! For whosoever shall do the will of God, the same is my brother, and my sister, and mother (Mark 3:31-35)**

Elijah and Elisha knew their purpose of connection. God wanted the successive prophetic anointing sustained in the earth. It was God who picked the person for Elijah. Just as a father cannot choose his order of sons, or the sex of his child, neither can he randomly select the chosen son to carry his mantle. For God wants whom he wants. Elijah couldn't remain in the earth forever. God wanted to use him for a specific period of time. And that time was almost over, but the anointing of Elijah was not! So Elisha carried Elijah's anointing further in the generations to come. It is even clear how Malachi prophesied that another man would receive the anointing of Elijah, post Elisha's usage of it:

**Behold, I will send you Elijah the prophet before the coming of the great and dreadful day of the Lord: and he shall turn the heart of the fathers to the children, and the heart of the children to their fathers, lest I come and smite the earth with a curse (Malachi 4:5-6).**

- And Jesus Christ proclaims that this prophecy was fulfilled through the life of John the Baptist:

**Verily I say unto you, among them that are born of women there hath not risen a greater than John the Baptist...and if ye will receive it, this is Elijah, which was for to come" (Matthew 11:11a, 14).**

- When Jesus was in Caesarea Philippi, you can see the teaching of the protocols of the passing of the prophetic mantle of the prophetic father of the prophetic group was still in motion:

**When Jesus came into the coasts of Caesarea Philippi, he asked his disciples, saying, Whom do men say that I the Son of man am? And they said, some say that thou art John the Baptist: some, Elijah; and others, Jeremiah, or one of the prophets (Matthew 16:13-14).**

When reviewing this storyline, some information was misappropriated. People were spreading rumors that John was one of the prophets. This misappropriation is more seen when some of the apostles responded with saying John was likened unto the spirit of other former prophets from the Old Testament. Their error brings about an even greater implication. And that implication reveals the successive anointing of the prophets of Old is a process that is passed down through the generations. Jesus skillfully dealt with the misconception of the teachings of the Scribes by explaining his own pending testimony of the prophetic suffering that was to come:

***And His disciples asked him, saying, why then say the scribes that Elijah must first come? And Jesus answered and said unto them, Elijah truly shall first come, and restore all things. But I say unto you, that Elijah is come already, and they knew him not, but have done unto him whatsoever they listed. Likewise shall also the Son of man suffer of them. Then the disciples understood that he spake unto them of John the Baptist. (Matthew 17:10-13).***

When you look at the three prophetic generations of the Old Testament, you see a strange emergence. Instead of Moses' two natural sons becoming prophetic successors, the anointing of leadership went to Joshua. But the prophetic sonship was upon Aaron and Miriam. Miriam and Aaron were Moses' older siblings, but in the spirit they were Moses' spiritual children. Both died before Moses, leaving no clear prophetic son to take on his mantle post his death.

When you revisit the lineage of the band of prophets, there are major prophetic generations spawned. However, the successor of those generations does not come from the Levitical line. It appeared that King David of the tribe of Judah was destined to become the prophetic son of Samuel (Acts 2:30). This is solely possible because of Samuel and David's working relationship. God sent Samuel to anoint David as king, but it was a prophetic anointing upon Samuel's life that transferred into David's life (1 Samuel 16:13). David shows Samuel's anointing during his functioning as an honorary Levite with a prophetic spirit. Even though he was called to kingship, David reproduced a Levitical reality within the temple and palaces:

**All these which were chosen....these were reckoned by their genealogy in their villages, whom David and Samuel the seer did ordain in their set office. (1 Chronicles 9:22).**

The order of transition is proper within their storyline. Samuel died before David, and David carried Samuel's prophetic leadership blessing further into the earth. It was not solely of a Levitical assignment for David as much as it was a kingly one. As a result of Samuel's death, the band of prophets' era diminished. The strongest survival of them all is seen in the successive anointing of the Elijah and Elisha paradigm. All roads met again with Levi and Judah when Joseph and Mary joined in marriage. From their marriage and God's miracle, Jesus was born. So the importance of the prophetic family and the proper functionality of prophetic succession are just as important as Rabbinical and Apostolic Successions. Just as it was important to Adam and his sons, for every son needs a father. And every father needs a son. This is equally true for prophetic people.

## The Correlation of Spiritual Adoption & Prophetic Sons

Elijah and Elisha's paradigm brings us to a correlation of not just prophetic fathering and sonship adoption scenarios, but it presents the spiritual adoption for all God's children. When God created the human family, He created the very first super ministry in scripture. It is the basis of all ministerial, ecclesiastical and spiritual concepts that we use in even today's church. The Apostle Paul clarified that the usage of such family titles is the proper respect due to family members within the body of Christ:

**Rebuke not an elder, but entreat him as a father; and the younger men as brethren; the elder women as mothers; the younger as sisters, with all purity (1 Timothy 5:1-2).**

The roles are defined. He calls them fathers, mothers, brothers and sisters. Just as the natural family is established, so is the supernatural family. This phenomenon is also called the household of faith (Galatians 6:10) and the household of God (Ephesians 2:19). Many people get it very confused. For even the word church doesn't start in the New Testament, but rather begins in the Old Testament. Israel was the first mega-church, and the Children of Israel were called the church in the wilderness (Acts 7:38 - KJV). "Family" and "church" are used in both Testaments.

And this family structure and first church all began with the two individuals we call Adam and Eve, the parents of all men and prophets. Every son needs a family, father and a place to call home. When Paul wrote to his churches, he even saw them as his children:

*I write not these things to shame you, but as my beloved sons I warn you. For though ye have ten thousand instructors in Christ, yet have ye not many fathers: for in Christ Jesus have I begotten you through the gospel. Wherefore I beseech you, be ye followers of me. For this cause have I sent unto you Timotheus, who is my beloved son, and faithful in the Lord, who shall bring you into remembrance of my ways which be in Christ, as I teach everywhere in every church (1 Corinthians 4:14-17).*

Spiritual parents are the byproduct of the original family! If there are apostolic, prophetic and pastoral fathers, their origins will certainly find greater purpose by reviewing the original family of God. For Paul told the church of Corinth how Timothy was in fact his spiritual son. Again, you cannot have sonship without fatherhood. And you cannot have fatherhood without genealogy. So the aspects of the human family have many parallelisms. As Adam created the first human generation, Levi created the first prophetic generation. All believers are family members through the adoptive process of God:

*For as many as are led by the Spirit of God, they are the sons of God. For ye have not received the spirit of bondage again to fear; but ye have received the Spirit of adoption, whereby we cry, Abba, Father. The Spirit itself beareth*

**witness with our spirit, that we are the children of God (Romans 8:14-16).**

Even Jesus released the spirit of adoption during his final moments of his crucifixion. Instead of using one of his blood relatives or siblings, he nominated his best friend, John in becoming his mother's son. This process of instantaneous adoption is the same process a spiritual child of God experiences the moment they receive Jesus Christ as their Lord and Savior:

**Now there stood by the cross of Jesus his mother, and his mother's sister, Mary the wife of Cleophas, and Mary Magdalene. When Jesus therefore saw his mother, and the disciple standing by, whom he loved, he saith unto his mother, Woman, behold thy son! Then saith he to the disciple, Behold thy mother! <u>And from that hour that disciple took her unto his own home (John 19:25-27, KJV)</u>.**

John instantly takes Jesus' mother as his mother on that day at the bottom of the cross. We, too, can instantly become part of Jesus's divine family because of our belief in his atoning work on the cross. It's an immediate transaction just as John did with Mary, the Mother of Jesus. He instantly accepted her from that day forward as a member of his own home and family. What's interesting to note is that Mary's other naturally born children are part of the first believers after Jesus' resurrection. What's also important to note is that Jude was on the discipleship team. But regardless of those other truths, the power of adoption outweighed other family members. God says in this, He wants what He wants when He wants it. And the good news is that God wants us to become part of his eternal family through the adoption that is in Christ Jesus.

Therefore, our prophetic correlation to this general biblical teaching is through God's divine plan of the prophetic adoption of spiritual sons through Jesus Christ's atoning work at Calvary's cross unto a prophetic house that is governed by Him. But we must first accept that we are even sons:

*Having predestined us unto <u>the adoption of children by Jesus Christ to Himself</u>, according to the good pleasure of His will (Ephesians 1:5, KJV)*

*To redeem them that were under the law, that we might receive <u>the adoption of sons</u>. And because ye are son, God hath sent forth the Spirit of His Son into your hearts, crying, Abba, Father (Galatians 4:4-5, KJV).*

*He was in the world, and the world was made by Him, and the world knew Him not. He came unto His own, and His own received Him not. But as many as received Him, to them gave He power to become the Sons of God, even to them that believe on His name: which were born, not of blood, nor of the will of the flesh, nor of the will of man, but of God (John 1:10-13, KJV).*

*Behold, what manner of love the Father hath bestowed upon us, that <u>we should be called the sons of God</u>: therefore the world knoweth us not, because it knew Him not. Beloved, <u>now are we the sons of God</u>, and it doth not yet appear what we shall be: but we know that, when we shall appear, <u>we shall be like him</u>; for we shall see Him as He is (1 John 3:1-2, KJV).*

## A Prophetic Father's Words Over His Prophetic Son

The emergence of prophetic fathers and sons is not a new paradigm for the New Testament alone. It actually is an Old Testament Origin. John the Baptist and his very own father, Zechariah were the first pattern of prophetic family within the New Testament:

**And his father Zecharias was filled with the Holy Ghost, and prophesied, saying...And thou, child, shalt be called the prophet of the Highest: for thou shalt go before the face of the Lord to prepare his ways (Luke 1:67, 76).**

Zechariah was a Kohathite Levite by the course of Abijah (Luke 1:5), who was a descendent of Aaron (1 Chronicles 24:1, 10). Aaron was not only a high priest, but he was a prophet of God to the ministry of his brother Moses (Exodus 7:1). It was a common theme for a patriarch of the Jewish race to become prophetic at random periods of their life. Take, for example, Jacob and his prophetic discourse to his 12 sons on his death bed (Genesis 49:1-28).

These genetic reminders are confirmation to the spiritual revelations that there are still prophetic generations: some genetic and some God-given. Regardless of their generation's orientation, the need for prophetic families need to emerge for the safety of the prophetic gift and office which truly remains. Even when Paul was speaking to Timothy, he told him that it was the prophetic words spoken over his life by him and the prophetic presbytery that would sustain him and his destiny:

***This charge I commit unto thee, son Timothy, according to the prophecies which went before on thee, that thou by them mightest war a good warfare (1 Timothy 1:18).***

***Neglect not the gift that is in thee, which was given thee by prophecy, with the laying on of the hands of the presbytery (1 Timothy 4:14)***

***Wherefore I put thee in remembrance that thou stir up the gift of God, which is in thee by the putting on of my hands (2 Timothy 1:6)***

Only the power of a spiritual father has the ability to shape the identity of a spiritual son. This working relationship between father and son comes through tutelage of sound teaching and discipleship. It is a practical reality. If the student doesn't usurp authority and remains faithful to his father's teaching, then the benefit of what that the father possesses will one day become transmitted unto the son. When Paul used Timothy to go to various churches, it was because of the strong discipleship program he had with his spiritual son:

***I write not these things to shame you, but as my beloved sons I warn you. For though ye have ten thousand instructors in Christ, yet have ye not many fathers: for in Christ Jesus I have begotten you through the gospel. Wherefore I beseech you, be ye followers of me. For this cause have I sent unto you Timotheus, who is my beloved son, and faithful in the Lord, who shall bring you into remembrance of my ways which be in Christ, as I teach everywhere in every church (1 Corinthians 4:11-17)***

The faithfulness in connecting and training of a son towards their father and the father's love and nurturing to their son will produce a truly subsequent prophetic generation. It takes time, love, and commitment. Legitimacy releases authenticity. The power of prophecy shapes identity. When Zechariah spoke over John the Baptist, like Paul spoke over Timothy, it brings us back to the Old Testament example of Jacob, speaking over his sons (Genesis 49). For Jacob (Israel) prophesied over his sons just as all current prophetic fathers should. For a prophetic father's words are very important to the prophetic survival of his son's future in ministry.

This is why it's important to not confuse pastoring with prophetic-parenting. For there are many times when the children are prophetic and the parent is not. When this occurs, there needs to be a viable connection with a prophetic team who are trustworthy to cover other households of prophetic citizens. When I think of this reality, a direct scripture comes to mind. It's the story of Philip the Evangelist. He has four daughters who are prophetesses. They are his blood children who he also pastors while literally living under his very roof.

And it is quite possible that the Judean-Christian prophet, Agabus, was a prophetic spiritual father to Philips' natural daughters. This is highly speculative, but not unlikely. Philip was a pastor by default because he had a household filled with people. Those people were all Christians and blood relatives. Philip's call is to the office of the Evangelist and not the prophet. Therefore, it was a peculiar connectivity of having a father who is evangelistic and authentically pastoral but not prophetic:

***And the next day we that were of Paul's company departed, and came unto Caesarea: and we entered into the house of Philip the evangelist, which was one of the seven; and abode with him. And the same man had four daughters, virgins which did prophesy. And as we tarried there many days, there came down from Judea a certain prophet, named Agabus (Acts 21:8-10).***

Unsupervised prophetic workers and self-assumed prophets are a major liability within the body of Christ. We need the return of prophetic houses that have capable fathers and mothers who are prophetic leaders. Leaders that have seasoned words to speak over their prophetic children like Zecharias did with John. Even prophetic uncles and aunts are needed. For a prophetic house without a prophetic leader is a house that will need some type of prophetic government. If it were not so, the scripture would not reflect such a truth. Philip's house is of no exception or exemption.

This raises another important point. Is the kingdom challenging the credentials and origins of the emerging prophets of this current generation? Do we have any modern day Gibeah's, Ramah's and sober minded people like Amos asking whose house do you prophetically come from? For who is the prophetic father, mentor or leader? And what prophetic place does their credentials and developments come from? If you don't have those answers in proper alignment, then you are in danger of the tragedy and abomination of improper prophetic performance.

A prophet without an origin is dangerous. Many rise without any accountability, which surfaces another question: Where are the true prophetic fathers and mothers? Just as much as we need the survival of the prophetic generations, there is no guarantee of survival of prophetic mantles if we don't have the presence of the prophetic parent. The son is looking for the father to speak well over them, so that the son can become all he can be in the kingdom of God.

The absence of this paradigm is the very reason there is so much demonic attack against the gift of prophecy. We can fully understand how these attacks become so great upon the prophetic and those assigned to prophetic generations. In some respects, we are walking with a lack of knowledge in this subject matter. And because of abuse, misuse and lack of understanding, the church and kingdom of God have become weary and leery of the operation of such a beautiful gift.

Even worse among prophetic people is the great displacement. Prophetic people certainly are in need of an environment to grow. They can't find a suitable prophetic home to learn how to cultivate, and thus exercise their gifting. This is why most prophetic people are dismissing their gift. They have decided to allow its dormancy out of respect for God. With reverential fear of hurting the church and the people of God, they abstain from the prophetic altogether.

The office of such an anointing is present within the lives of many people. The search for a sober prophetic place is over! It is over if the prophetic fathers and mothers would emerge. For every child needs a parent, and parents are nothing without children. The two entities of the prophetic family must find each other and function properly therein. And the roles of such operations are surely necessary.

Additionally, we have many improperly thinking that prophetic fathering and mothering means an opportunity of enslavement. The parent knows their entire purpose is to develop and deposit proper directives into their children and it is the job of the parent to seek and salvage the efforts of their spiritual children—not the other way around:

*"...And I will not be burdensome to you: for I seek not yours, but you: for the children ought not to lay up for the parents, but the parents for the children. And I will very gladly spend and be spent for you..." (2 Corinthians 12:14b, 15a).*

Prophetic fathering is not an opportunity to Lord over sons making them mere slaves (1 Peter 5:3). Neither is it an opportunity for sons to become disobedient, afflicting the hearts of true fathers. And equally it is unadvisable for spiritual fathers to be inconsistent towards the development of their spiritual children. If this perpetration is allowed, then the end result will be the letting down and extensive hurt of one's sons. For the Bible exhorts the way children must honor their natural fathers according to the 10 commandments. And the word also commands that natural fathers remain charged to honor their natural children. Spiritual children and spiritual fathers must follow this same protocol when dealing with each other within their designated spiritual family:

*Children, obey your parents in the Lord: for this is right. Honor thy father and mother: which is the first commandment with promise; that it may be well with thee, and thou mayest live long on the earth. And, ye fathers, provoke not your children to wrath: but bring them up in the nurture and admonition of the Lord (Ephesians 6:1-4).*

# 7

# The Goal is God!

## MY PROPHETIC GENERATION
### The Revelation of the New Prophetic Generations
*Psalm 78:4-8*

It was my deepest desire to be very transparent about the process of my testimony. Before I could share revelation, I wanted to establish more credibility. And I wanted to show you the truth about being imperfect beings called to a perfected work. For the work of the prophetic ministry is a very sensitive and serious process. The prophetic requires the utmost integrity and proper training. The reason being is very clear. Prophets are currently considered heretics and a hoax by many believers who don't understand the current manifestation of what is truly prophetic. Another major concern is the presence of the spirit of error which operates among unlearned but true prophetic mantles. One area of error is some prophet's function from a series of poorly learned behaviors. These poor behaviors are taught to them from other unlearned prophets, or they minister to the level of their incomplete biblical and spiritual immaturity or subjective denominationalism. And their assertion of this gifting is usually done with an anger and hostility coupled with an Old Testament mentality. It is certainly time for the prophet to function more like a New Testament prophet should.

Instead of a mature, sound and competent oracle, there is a propensity to inaccurately represent God and His voice. So the vision and call for prophetic reformation is very obvious. The good news is that there is a new generation emerging with suitable scriptural education and expression. This new generation has the kingdom mandate to operate on a higher level of prophetic proficiency. The Lord is sanctifying and sanitizing the apostolic and prophetic anointing. And He is requiring that each prophetic generation increase with knowledge while the former generation must impart wisdom into the next generation:

**We will not hide them from their children, showing to the generation to come the praises of the Lord, and His strength, and His wonderful works that He hath done. For He established a testimony in Jacob, and appointed a law in Israel, which He commanded our fathers, that they should make them known to their children: That the generation to come might know them, even the children which should be born; who should arise and declare them to their children: that thy might set their hope in God, and not forget the works of God, but keep His commandments: And might not be as their fathers, a stubborn and rebellious generation; a generation that set not their heart aright, and**

**whose spirit was not steadfast with God (Psalm 78:4-8, KJV).**

A distinct clause from this pericope says the goal of each previous generation is to teach their subsequent generation *not to forget the works of God* (Psalm 78:7b)! And because I have been exposed to this mandate, I, too, have accepted the calling of ensuring that this new prophetic generation is properly trained with the purpose of improving and releasing even greater prophetic impartations into other generations. Surely the devil wants to keep the revelation of the prophetic family paradigm fragmented, perverted and ineffective. Satan wants to greatly displace the prophetic gifting from the original purposes and assignments that were originally intended to be fulfilled. That is why the enemy is trying to erase the prophetic anointing altogether.

• • •

1985-1995 primarily were the years of working out my soul salvation and coming into the knowledge of my prophetic assignment. Through trial and errors, heartaches and pain before my first ten-year cycle ended, I was officially introduced to preaching ministry. And from 1995-2005, I would understand this period as the time for me to work on the much that was given. It was the era of development concerning my prophetic ability. This was the time that I had to learn the scriptures and privately practice what God has said. But now I am called within this third semester of life (from 2005-2015) to articulate the depths of this revelation concerning the emerging of a new prophetic generation. And the last in-part prophecy I have received, so far, is that of 2015-2025; I believe

God will have me to travel the world to help churches establish the return of prophetic communities.

My personal roadway of becoming an apostolic voice, prophetic father and didactic leader is validated. I'm called to assist only those who have the appetite for this revelation and this book will serve as an evangelistic summons unto those who are striving to be sober, sane and sincere prophetic people of God. This book also is a means of globally connecting with others who share my sentiments and heartstrings for the advancement of God's kingdom. It is my commission to see credentialing and credibility of the prophet and prophetic gift properly restored.

The revelations and rhema in this book is gleaned from the word and time that I've spent with the Spirit of God. God has released this book to you through His predestinated plan. This prophetic burden has become ever increasing the older I become within this assignment. So I say to those of you who are searching for clarity, take this book and read it with all scrutiny.

## Decrees and Declarations: Final Thoughts

The natural generations of the Bible have recorded families. They possess designating vocations such as shepherds, warriors, artists, and kings. The same is with a generation of a particular family who produces the natural bloodline of the chosen people called to birth prophets. And the very fact that you picked up this book and purchased it can be a blatant confirmation that you're prophetically going in the right direction.

The fusing scriptures with my revelations from the Old and New Testaments was to teach on the importance of finding your prophetic place, family and generation. The easy part was reading this material, but the major task is placed within your hands to accomplish such findings. So the mandate is clear. Every prophetic person needs to find their prophetic home. For in it, resides your victory and validity.

In my second book, *The Doctrine of Prophecy*, we discover the biblical fundamentals assigned for every prophet to function therein. I hope that you seek this book as well. Combining the two will sustain you as you diligently seek the place assigned to launch your prophetic destiny.

As a master prophetic intercessor and watchmen, I have accepted my charge to decree and declare, under my apostolic mantle, the necessary prophetic triages for the church and kingdom. So I summarize this book with these important thoughts:

## **Prophetic Declaration #1**

I convey to you that the prophetic mantles of God must be properly released among the ultimate prophetic generation of Jesus Christ. There is no other generation that a New Testament prophet can function. For Jesus Christ is the Master and Father of all True Prophets. And all true prophets must submit their allegiance to His generation and prophetic genealogy. Furthermore, we, who are prophetic, are called to reside in the exclusive prophetic family of God which was created by Jesus Christ. And we are surely governed by chief elders who have been confirmed and affirmed to prophetically father us. But at the appointed time we must take on the responsibility of prophetically fathering others.

The assignment of the office and gifting of the prophet, under a true spirit of prophecy, is generational and no longer an individualized assignment. Never has there been prophetic exclusivity within this dispensation and time. John the Baptist was the last of the individualized prophets birthed and developed alone and apart from the prophetic body and Christian community. For all prophets must surely connect to a prophetic environment, leader and family to grow therein. I decree and declare all nomad prophets will one day soon become labeled as literal prophetic abominations by the body of Christ.

**Prophet Joel clairvoyantly uttered this revelation:**

*And ye shall know that I am in the midst of Israel, and that I am the Lord your God, and none else: and my people shall never be ashamed. And it shall come to pass afterward, that I will pour out my spirit upon all flesh: and your sons and daughters shall prophesy, your old men shall dream dreams, your young men shall see visions: and also upon the servants and upon the handmaids in those days will I pour out my spirit (Joel 2:27-29).*

<u>Apostle Peter confirmed that the flow was released and continues from its first day, which starts at Pentecost:</u>

*But Peter, standing up with the eleven, lifted up his voice, and said unto them, Ye men of Judea, and all ye that dwell at Jerusalem, be this known unto you, and hearken to my words: for these are not drunken, as ye suppose, seeing it is but the third hour of the day. But this is that which was spoken by the prophet Joel;*

*And it came to pass in the last days, saith God, I will pour out of my Spirit upon all flesh: and your sons and your daughters shall prophesy, and your young men shall see visions, and your old men shall dream dreams: and on my servants and on my handmaidens I will pour out in those days of my Spirit; and they shall prophesy (Acts 2:14-18, KJV).*

**This is why I prophetically speak:**

God is rebuilding the chosen prophetic generation of Jesus Christ through those who have been adopted into the family of God. Those who have accepted the testimony of Jesus Christ will not only accept salvation but the spirit of prophecy.

The return of under-master prophets, known as prophetic fathers, will serve as proxy reminders of a prophet's commitment to their ultimate prophetic father, Jesus Christ!

Being that Jesus Christ is the only destined head and patriarch of the current flow for the prophetic anointing, we look for no other master prophetic father. He is the final prophetic father, and we accept that we all are in the final prophetic generation. For the last prophetic generation will exist during the tribulation period, and when this period is over, the prophetic family will dissolve. But I decree and declare now that the New Prophetic Generation of Jesus Christ must fully emerge within His Holy Kingdom!

**Further Prophetic Revelation:**

The family of prophets' paradigm is now the current revelation God wants to use among the current prophets of the New Testament Church. Their true title is the Latter-Day New Testament Prophets.

## Prophetic Declaration #2

All prophets and prophetic people must come into some formal school, guild or training center to ensure the legitimacy and proper functionality of their gifting and office. The reprimand and indictment towards the church is clear. God is calling all churches to find or produce places designated for these specifically gifted in the prophetic. And God is rebuilding and reforming the prophetic capitals for a proper environment for the emergence of the current release of today's prophetic people.

Moreover, I decree and declare, in the name of Jesus, that prophetic fathers and mothers will emerge again to ensure proper Christian discipleship and nurturing of this said gift. This revelation is heavily connected to the biblical understanding as to how God originally released the revelation of the prophetic anointing within the earth's realm:

Sons, daughters, fathers, and mothers will experience the prophetic grace and anointing during the current church age. That is why Paul, the apostle, calls it the greatest gift to covet:

***But covet earnestly the best gifts: and yet show I unto you a more excellent way (1 Corinthians 12:31)***

***Follow after charity, and desire spiritual gifts, but rather that ye may prophesy....Wherefore, brethren, covet to prophesy...." (1 Corinthians 14:1,39a, KJV).***

Therefore, the church must unite and become a conglomerate in the Spirit (as a prophetic family) once again, just as the natural family is viable and a vicious force, created and assigned to destroy the plans of the enemy. All believers who are prophetic must accept that this supernatural calling and anointing is sent by God, exclusively through Jesus Christ!

## Prophetic Declaration #3

God's first major use of a family as a generation to do a great prophetic work was through the prophetic generations that were birthed out of the fourth generation of the sons of Levi.

This generation stems from the founding father of that generation whose name is Kohath. It is from Kohath's lineage that God revealed that the prophetic should be released through a family-oriented paradigm. And the revelation of this paradigm is termed by the patriarch of that generation:

## **Prophetic Declaration #4**

The Kohathite anointing is returning to the world through the body of Christ! It is biblically proven and should be biblically adhered in its proper functionality. The Lord has given this book as a means of ensuring that we will not walk in ignorance concerning the spiritual gift and the official governmental office of the prophet.

## Conclusion

The vision of God shows that there is too much division, within the prophetic, among those who are by faith and by the spirit. It is time to sober. And let us then employ biblical fundamentals, revelations and protocols as a means of providing a current prophetic government. We should further engage all prophets and prophetic workers with these mandates to ensure accuracy and accountability. This book has been called to enlighten and provide curricula for further and future development towards our advancement of the prophetic.

The approach was one of universality and not a dogmatic doctrinal approach. We are not here to satisfy denominational jurisdictions. It is the personal objective of each organization to glean what they deem applicable and necessary for their organization. This book wasn't written to attack any present denomination who is subjectively exercising the prophetic gift, but to be a tool of *iron sharpening iron*, provoking more intellectual strategy with spiritual wisdom! The prayer is that this book enhances the already prophetic and awakens the prophetically inactive—regardless of denomination! This work is present and must be properly accounted for. You and I, who assume such a calling, is held highly responsible for continual and proper usage.

The protocols that Paul instilled within Corinth and the other epistles, along with the words of Christ and the Apostles should be considered our current prophetic creed. And our prophetic creed should be coupled with the wise literature of the Old Covenant because it is in those annals that we glean fundamentals and advancements to procure suitable prophetic revelations. Certainly, this raises the bar for those who assert themselves or practices on any level the prophetic.

The current manifestation of the prophetic is without excuse and certainly shouldn't have as much compromise as it has been infamously known for. Unfortunately, this book cannot contain every prophetic prospective. However, these few nuggets gleaned can help strengthen the present and possible prophetic works within the body of Christ. Neither is the book the sole remedy for all prophetic problems. However, I pray that some of the current prophetic disgraces of the church can be treated from God's point of view given through me to you.

I have journeyed from simplicity to complexity on the subject of prophecy as a means of directly identifying what God has placed within my spirit and upon my heart. He is truly pulling me into the clear revelation that there is a current operation of the prophetic. Thus, the goal of this book was not to be just another book of catchall phrases or quick clichés that will leave a temporary or only a slight impression.

I apostolically assert that *the time of prophetic misrepresentation is over!* The hoax about prophesying is soon to reach its death and end. Moreover, the spirit of error concerning the prophetic is near its eradication. We, who are truly prophetic, are now called to raise our level of understanding while corresponding with our privilege of becoming better in our maturity, mentality, and even being more spiritually sound when it comes to being prophetic.

For man must certainly realize that the days of man are only for a brief moment. The word declares that when night comes no man can work. Therefore, each generational assignment unto the prophetic comes with urgency and no room for delay. The genealogies of scripture do matter and they have stronger implications. And not just for mere decoration. Our current generational assignment is in the gleaning of the foundational knowledge and wisdom of the Old Testament. With prayer, this will enhance the mantles and paradigms of the Latter-Day New Testament Prophet.

So I ask you, my dear reader: Have you found your prophetic purpose? Have you found your prophetic capital? Have you found your prophetic father? And do you understand what you must do in order to grow prophetically?

There are so many questions that have to be answered and very little time for any of us to find. Therefore, it is our responsibility that we don't allow this gift to fall to the ground and remain in a place of displacement and darkness of ignorance. We must stand up and not allow this gift to be continually disrespected by the devil. For the lack of knowledge and the spirit of the enemy are the reasons and causes of such negative infiltrations of the prophetic within God's church and kingdom.

There is now a greater and discernible generation who is taking their prophetic assignment more seriously than ever! And it appears that their sincerity is just as visible as the former prophets and guilds. Beloved, see this book as an assignment of development and a prophetic burden! See the importance of a prophetic generation working with its next generation:

*We will not hide them from their children, showing to the generation to come the praises of the Lord, and His strength, and His wonderful works that He hath done. For He established a testimony in Jacob, and appointed a law in Israel, which He commanded our fathers, that they should make them known to their children: That the generation to come might know them, even the children which should be born; who should arise and declare them to their children: that thy might set their hope in God, and not forget the works of God, but keep His commandments: And might not be as their fathers, a stubborn and rebellious generation; a generation that set not their heart aright, and whose spirit was not steadfast with God (Psalm 78:4-8, KJV).*

This integrity is gradually returning to the prophetic works within the church and kingdom because God is still on His mission of coming back for a church without spot or wrinkle. And since the Latter-Day New Testament Prophet is a part of the five-fold ministry, sent to assist with Christ's mission, the prophet is about reformation of the people through its prophetic ministry.

Hopefully this book will place the same burden of learning upon you. I pray that you have now become more interested in dissecting this information as a means of enhancing true placement within the New Prophetic Generation of Kohath. Furthermore, we have an even greater responsibility of accountability because we have the capability of learning more and expressing more of the greater works that Jesus declares. The word of God firmly teaches us that every work; or shall we say every preordained—good and faithful—work should be greater in quantity until the Lord returns:

**Verily, verily, I say unto you, He that believeth on me, the works that I do he do also; and greater works than these shall he do, because I go unto my Father (John 14:12, KJV).**

So the source of the prophetic work being the greatest, or superlative of gifts, has never been for the benefit of mankind to be glorified. But its presence is for the furtherance of the glorification of God unto the day and completion of the testimony of Jesus Christ. However, we shouldn't feel slighted or stifled in our approach of taking on the unique mantles and purposes of prophecy as we strive to advance it unto the next levels.

The Bible is still the blueprint of all prophetic authorization. It is the measuring stick and the exclusive manual of creativity for the expressions of revelation done by the prophetic gift. That is why there isn't anything wrong with the creation of prophetic schools as a means of clarifying order to the clarion voice of God within the lives of a prophetic people. God desires this revelation to be reproduced in the earth; the scriptures indicate such a clear design with the former five schools and even the cities of Rome, Thessalonica, Antioch, Corinth, and Ephesus, serving as our newest prophetic paradigms.

My deepest prayer is that those who may encounter this book will see the burden of the Lord in maintaining a higher integrity of the gift and office of the prophet. I pray that my testimony and revelations concerning the prophetic will inspire future generations to come and that this book becomes a guideline for other pastors and emerging prophetic fathers. For we certainly need the prophet and the prophetic gift throughout the church era.

We, too, are likened unto the prophets of Abraham, Enoch, and the family of Levi with Moses, Miriam, Aaron, and the prophetic works of Isaiah, Jeremiah and Malachi, even the great prophetic presence of Simeon, Anna, and John the Baptist. The only difference is they served as our great and prophetic forefathers and foremothers, but we now have to become them—for once they were us.

We, too, can have New Bethels, Ramahs, Gilgals, Jerichos, and even Gibeahs. We, too, have to govern New Corinth, Antioch, or Thessalonian, Roman and Ephesian churches. For these moments of scripture consistently teach us that whether our ministry is local, national or international, the integrity of the prophet is highly important. The prophetic network that we belong to is equally important to uphold.

That is why we need a prophetic place for a prophetic people. The proper nurturing of the prophetic is surely important. Just as you would develop your natural children, who are created with uniqueness, we need to foster an environment of freedom and void of condemnation for those who assert, through faith, the gift and spirit of prophecy. These guidelines protect the error of the prophetic and the misrepresentation of God in whom the true prophet speaks. It is with urgency that we reach out to the masses with a new approach of prophesying under grace and not calamity with interpersonal development of mutual prophetic accountability. I am clear that God sits on the throne of His glory in the heights of the heavens declaring, decreeing and determining that mankind will respect the office and gift of prophecy.

Prophesying was created for man's lethargic approach of worship unto the true and living God. And now that prophesying, prophecy and the office of the prophet are here, we must now embrace, educate and engage synonymously with the testimony of Jesus Christ. This is where prophecy begins and will end. Jesus Christ is the validation of the return of the Kohath anointing amongst the New Testament church.

**"...For the Spirit of Prophecy is the Testimony of Jesus Christ" (Revelation 19:10b)**

So let's walk in the Kohath anointing of Jesus and be the true prophetic family of God! Let the New Prophetic Generation emerge!

# About Apostle Sherman D. Farmer

**Apostle Sherman D. Farmer** is a visionary and prophet entrusted with the vision of God to shepherd millions of souls into the kingdom. Over 20 years, his soul-saving messages have reached the hearts of men and women throughout the world. Apostle Farmer's distinct and unparalleled ability to impart training of integrity through the compassion, empowerment and inspiration of the Holy Spirit has caused his ministry to flourish.

Founder of The New Apostolic Prophetic Reformation of the United and Covenanted Churches, a subsidiary of the New Gibeah Ministries for Christ, Inc. and Straightway Apostolic

Ministries located in Capitol Heights, Maryland, he also serves as the Chief Apostle to Redeeming Touch of Love. Helping prophets establish and fully develop proper functioning of their gifts through biblical and doctrinal aptitude courses, he is the founding visionary of the New Kohath Prophetic Institute.

He is also the visionary behind several entities of ministry, including The NGMC Worship Center, a prophetic house of fellowship, worship, ministry, discipleship, and evangelism; The House of Benjamin Annex, bridging the gap between educational, vocational and secular systems; The Delores O. Farmer School for Christians in the Performing Arts, serving those gifted in theater, visual arts, music, dance and vocational arts; Straightway Ministries, imparting wisdom, knowledge and understanding in an instructional environment through an international outreach; and The NGMC School of Ministry, training ministers, pastors and other religious leaders in various areas.

Apostle Farmer is a renowned teacher and a highly sought after leader with life changing Bible study sessions including: The Prison Epistles, teaching believers how to work heavily in ministry under the stress of spiritual warfare; Project MAPP (Ministry Assignment Placement Program), providing believers with the tools to understand and identify their spiritual gifts; and The Life of Christ, equipping believers with the required full armor on the parables, historical timelines, genealogy and spirituality of Jesus Christ in order to become effective witnesses.

As an advocate for finding creative venues to reach millions of souls, Apostle Farmer has directed benefit concerts for guest artists from Yolanda Adams to B.J. Crosby. He has conducted seminars in the areas of praise and worship and art, praise and worship reformation training, and served as one of the campaign coordinators for the *40 Days of Purpose Program*. In 2000, he created the Band of Prophets Online Ministry, teaching spiritual leaders how to become a Five-Fold Kingdom Builder.

Apostle Farmer's primary apostolic assignment is to legitimize the prophetic and apostolic voice in today's spiritually deprived world. He is forming a revolution of spiritual revivals within the Body of Christ by encouraging leaders to become more transparent and accessible. As Apostle Farmer continues to lead the people of God to their destiny, he stands firmly on the words of Isaiah: *"Also, I heard the voice of the Lord, saying, Whom shall I send, and who will go for us? Then said I, Here I am; send me."* (Isaiah 6:8 KJV)

Connect with Apostle Farmer or Share Your Feedback on:

amazon.com
goodreads.com
barnesandnoble.com

**WWW.ABOUT.ME/SHERMANDFARMER**

## PUBLISHING GROUP

YOUR WRITING IS A *Sacred* GIFT.

*Your Words* are more than an unbound manuscript waiting to be released into the world. It's a soon-to-be executed *divine assignment*, which can only be delivered by you.

The way it looks, feels and impacts is a direct extension of who you were

**CREATED TO BE + DESIRE TO BECOME**

#TheGreatest

It's Time to Unleash Your Manuscript!

*Are you ready? #PublishYourGift*

**www.PurposelyCreatedPG.com**

CONNECT WITH US!

(866) 674-3340
Hello@PurposelyCreatedPG.com
Facebook :: Twitter :: Instagram @PublishYourGift

www.ingramcontent.com/pod-product-compliance
Lightning Source LLC
Chambersburg PA
CBHW050634160426
43194CB00010B/1662